I0197015

The Dog Ate My Lipstick and
My Houseplants Have Fleas...

Sanity Check

A Collection of Columns

SHARON SHORT

Published by Cornerstone Communications

Copyright © 2012 Sharon Short

All rights reserved.

ISBN: 0615642632
ISBN-13: 978-0615642635

DEDICATION

To David, Katherine, Gwen, Dad, Janice, myriad
friends, Cosmo, Cookie, Candy, Snickers, and all other
creatures (human and otherwise) who graciously accepted
playing a role in *Sanity Check*. I love you all.

.

CONTENTS

CONTENTS

ACKNOWLEDGMENTS

In 1999, I began writing, in addition to fiction, short essays that would lead to *Sanity Check*, my humorous lifestyle column that ran weekly from the beginning of 2002 through the middle of 2012 in the *Dayton Daily News*.

I sent those essays to Writers' Block, an occasional column in the *Dayton Daily News* open to submissions from local writers. Several were published (and some are included here). At the end of 2001, Life section editor Ron Rollins called me and asked if I'd like to write a weekly column for the newspaper. We are, he said, looking for a regular humorous female voice for our Life section, and we think that's you. Then he added: your column would run on Mondays.

I'm sure Ron thought I'd hung up, because I was, for once in my life, speechless. I thought, is this a joke? Writers don't get phone calls like that. Eventually, I found my literal voice (not to be confused with my literary voice as referenced above), and asked out loud, is this a joke? (I could be this blunt not just because I was truly stunned, but because Ron is also a friend. We met at the Antioch Writers' Workshop in 1990.) Ron assured me he wasn't kidding, and that, actually, my Writers' Block submissions (which I had done for fun and without any aspirations for my essays turning into a regular gig) had paved the way.

And so it was that in February 2002, *Sanity Check* debuted in the *Dayton Daily News*, appearing every Monday until June 4, 2012. (Well, I did take one Monday off in 2011 while I recovered from major surgery.)

While putting together this collection, I realized that over ten-plus years, I've published about 560 *Sanity Check* columns (counting the forerunners in Writers' Block). At an average of 580 words a column, that's 324,800 words... or about four novels-worth

I am forevermore grateful to Ron, now Associate Editor of the *Dayton Daily News*, for giving me this opportunity. And I am thankful for all the *Dayton Daily News* editors who had a hand in editing my column over the years, each a joy to work with: Jana Collier, Connie Post, Alexis Larson, Michelle Fong, and Bob Underwood.

Thank you to all my family members and friends who graciously accepted appearing in my column.

A special thank you to Katherine (a.k.a., the older/brown-eyed daughter) and Gwen (a.k.a., the younger/blue-eyed daughter) for being good sports about appearing in your mom's column for most of your childhood, your adolescence, and on into your young adult years. And an extra thank you to Gwen for organizing the piles of copies and print outs of all of my columns. This collection would not have been possible without your help.

And finally, thank you to my readers. I've enjoyed your feedback, in emails, letters, and in person. It's always a joy when I find out that by sharing a bit of myself through my writing, I've touched someone else's life.

I hope you enjoy this collection of 100 of my and my readers' favorite *Sanity Check* columns.

Sharon Short
www.sharonshort.com
June 4, 2012

CHAPTER 1

~♥~

Trophy Wigs

Flush with conversation

There are mothers out there who complain that they can't get their kids to talk with them, but I don't understand that.

Frankly, I find it a cinch. All I have to do is go into the bathroom.

Picture yourself sitting in there with the door shut, looking for a little privacy—after all, your mother didn't raise you in a barn. Yet, a few rather personal moments later, the door swings open and there's your 6-year-old daughter, the one who at breakfast stared at the cereal box and hummed while you tried to talk with her about her friends, her shoes, her cat—anything.

Now she's staring at you, wide-eyed, but not because she's stumbled into the bathroom at a rather indelicate maternal moment. No, she's wide-eyed because she wants advice about how to extricate her little neighbor friend's parakeet from another little friend's dog's mouth. Unfortunately, she's brought the problem with her—dog, parakeet, both friends. All of whom are staring, too, wide-eyed (except the parakeet.) As you shove the door shut, you realize that the parakeet is just a stuffed toy—yet you're sure anyway that you can hear it moaning in a combination of terror and humiliation. You know just how the parakeet feels, too.

For some reason, this kind of thing doesn't seem to happen much to dads.

But the real problem for moms is not that these kind of things happen to us, but that we fail to see them as an opportunity. Yes, an opportunity!

Try this. Go into your bathroom. Lock the door. Run some tap water, hum a little. (This won't work if your kids think you're faking.) Before you know it, your children will have flocked outside the bathroom door, the little click of the lock being a Siren song to them. They will be hollering to you things such as, "Moira's got new pink sneakers. Can I get some too?" Or, "At lunch today, I traded that healthy tofu-on-rye sandwich you packed for me for a fried bologna burrito. Is that OK?"

Voila! Your kids are talking to you. Wasn't that easy?

2

The downside, of course, is that you'll find yourself limiting visits to the bathroom for actual reasons of nature to, say, when your kids are at school. During these times, the little dears' ears will perk up, but they will restrain themselves from running out of the building and coming back home. Or at least their teachers will restrain them. Most days. (I admit that summers, spring breaks and sick days are problematic with my method.)

However, there are other ways aside from the Bathroom Method. The Traffic Method, for instance.

I like to save my children's art projects—the ones they stuff to the bottom of their backpacks along with apple cores and rocks and damp socks. If I pull out the projects and coo over them at dinner and beg, "Please, oh, please tell me all about this," my kids just shrug and stare dumbly.

So, I've developed a new approach. Once I've collected several weeks' worth of drawings and clay pots and pipe-cleaner figurines, I load them and my kids into the back seat of my car. Then I take us for a drive, making sure that we get enmeshed into some really gnarly traffic.

Sure enough, soon my little dears are saying, "Mom, Mom, Mom! Turn around and look!" At that point, they'll carefully point out and discuss the various parts of the art project, in the order they made it..."

My kids still believe I do have eyes in the back of my head, so they think I'm really seeing all they're showing me. I'm having teeny-tiny video cams mounted in the back of my car next week, so I can watch later what they've so earnestly demonstrated. This isn't because driving and twisting to look in the back seat is a dangerous combination. This is because if I did turn around to look, they'd suddenly drop the stuff and stare out the windows.

You see, the trick to getting your kids to talk with you is to make them think you aren't really listening. And if you get in enough practice now, these diversionary tactics will continue to work for a lifetime. I envision myself, about 12 years from now, going into the bathroom with my portable phone receiver and locking the door. Turning on the tap water. Humming. Sure enough, the phone will ring. I'll answer, dewy-eyed with the knowledge that my kids aren't so busy with college or work or whatever that they can't spare a few precious moments to chat with dear old mom.

And they'll say, "Hi, mom. I'm kinda short on cash right now, so I was wondering..."

Hey, I never claimed my techniques would result in conversations that were actually interesting.
(May 28, 2000)

~♥~

Search for hobby becomes notable quest
I decided a few months ago that I needed a hobby.

At some spare moment—between family, work, and volunteer commitments—I realized I wasn't doing anything just for fun. Not that family, work, and volunteering aren't fun. But you know what I mean—I wasn't doing anything that was purely for fun. Purely for me. What's worse, it had been so long since I'd had a hobby, I had no ideas about what to try.

So I went to the experts: my family. My husband and two daughters represent at least six hobbies among them.

My husband (singing, soccer, painting) suggested that I take up cooking.

Uh huh.

So while we were eating dinner that night at a fast food restaurant, I asked my daughters (tae kwon do, soccer, computer games) what Mommy should do for a hobby. The darlings informed me I already had a hobby—cleaning the house.

Uh huh.

My hobby hunt suddenly became serious. After all, I couldn't let my daughters think the only "hobby" adult women have is housekeeping. So that night, while dusting the furniture, I tried to think up a hobby for myself. This proved more difficult than you might imagine.

For one thing, I don't like crafts. As a kid, I sewed right through my thumb in my junior high home economics class. So any kind of needlework was eliminated on the grounds of potential danger to myself and others.

And despite what my athletic husband and daughters try to tell me, I just don't see sports as a hobby. I view exercise as a health maintenance chore—like flossing.

Hardly hobby material. And as for sports... well, I like to *watch* games, but I have never been even remotely athletic. As a high school junior, I flunked the bowling portion of my gym-for-klutzes class.

Art or music seemed better hobby categories for me. So the next morning, I checked out art classes. I have an enduring sense that the sky will indeed fall if I fail to fulfill an obligation, so I knew I would attend an art class, thus being forced to keep up with a hobby. But the class time conflicted with my family, work, and volunteer commitments.

That left music. Music lessons are scheduled between teacher and student, so I figured I had a shot at finding time in my schedule for music. I studied piano as a kid, although I'd actually wanted to study clarinet. I checked with our occasional baby sitter—a teen who plays the clarinet—and she informed me that learning to play the saxophone would be easier.

Hmmm. The saxophone. Now *that* caught my fancy. I imagined myself casually saying to folks, "Hobbies? Oh yes, I have one. I play the saxophone." Wow! How cool! How hip! My daughters would never again think mommy's hobby was vacuuming! This would be fun!

So, I rented a sax. Arranged lessons. And found myself, on the way to my first lesson, completely horrified with what I was doing. Not because I doubted my choice of hobby. But because I knew there were paragraphs I needed to write. Laundry to fold. Committee meetings to prepare for. My enthusiasm for my fledgling hobby waned. How dare I take time away from my family, work and volunteering for something so... so... *unnecessary* as a hobby?

But I swallowed hard and went to my first lesson. I came home and started practicing. I kept practicing even when my daughters suggested that the basement, rather than the living room, would be a better setting. I kept practicing even when my cat stood by the window, howled, then finally clawed through the screen, jumped out, and ran under the deck where she hid for several hours.

At my next lesson, I learned that our clarinet-playing baby sitter is only partly right. The fingering on a saxophone is fairly simple. Getting the right tone is the challenging part. And breath support, my saxophone teacher explained to me, is essential to a good tone. He suggested some breathing exercises.

Driving home from my lesson, I thought carefully about what he'd said about breathing. And his advice brought to mind a seemingly discordant image: on airplanes, before takeoff, during the obligatory safety procedure demo, you're always told that if the oxygen masks drop down, take care of yourself first, and then help any small children who are with you. I understand the reasoning; yet I've always been mildly offended by it, because of course my first instinct would be to help my children.

But then, driving home from my saxophone lesson, the advice made more sense than ever. In an airplane emergency, I'd have to put that mask on first, because if I passed out, I couldn't help my children. And maybe the same was true of having a hobby—even one that drives my cat in panicky horror out the window.

(December 3, 2000)

~♥~

Chicken noodles ritual offers a recipe for life

I'm the sort of cook who has to check the back of the microwave popcorn bag for the recipe. Whose signature potluck dish is a plate of apple wedges—artfully arranged, of course.

So when I volunteer to help make homemade noodles for the annual chicken noodle dinner fund-raiser at our church, the ladies-who-always-make-the-noodles are, understandably, a little surprised. Still, being kind souls, they agree that I can help on noodle-making day.

I have an ulterior motive. I want their secret noodle recipe. The chicken noodles that the ladies of St. John's Lutheran Church in Miamisburg create once a year are, well, heavenly. For that know-how, I'm even willing to spend some learning time in a kitchen.

When I show up on noodle-making day, someone asks me, "Did you bring your rolling pin?"

8

"Rolling... pin...?" I repeat nervously. I have vague memories of seeing it in the kids' sand box once. "I need a rolling pin?"

"After you make the noodle dough," says the woman who will end up being my noodle-making mentor, "you have to roll it out, then slice the dough into noodles, then let them dry. You can use my rolling pin."

She hands it over and positions me in front of a lump of noodle dough.

"Just roll it as thin as a sheet of paper," my noodle-mentor advises. "But without ripping it."

How hard can that be? I smash down on the dough, roll as hard and fast as I can... and half the dough sticks to the pin, while the other half flings itself up and over the pin and onto the counter. Argh.

I start over with fresh dough, heeding my mentor's advice to add a little flour while rolling and to roll more gently.

After a while, I get the hang of it, enough to relax and listen as the ladies swap stories of how long they've had their rolling pins—some for as long as they've been married, 30 years or more. Some are on second or third rolling pins. I don't mention the location of my rolling pin. I just listen and roll.

The rolling pin stories lead to other stories... funny and sad, of triumphs and losses, some recent, some from long ago. From their stories, I realize these women know a lot more than a secret noodle recipe.

Eventually, I get the hang of rolling out noodles and am rewarded with getting to actually make noodle dough.

My mentor pushes a bowl, a scoop, two eggs and a bag of flour in front of me. I look around. Where's the recipe book? The secret list of ingredients? Measuring spoons and cups?

"Crack the two eggs into the bowl," my mentor instructs. "And add flour."

"How—how much?"

She shrugs. "About a cup."

I'm horrified. How much is about a cup? Nine-tenths? One and one 12th? "That's—that's it? *That's* the secret recipe?"

She laughs. "There's no secret recipe. Just add a cup of flour—enough so the dough looks and feels right when you start kneading it."

"But how will I know?

"Experience. After a while, you'll just know."

I scoop up some flour and put it in with the eggs. Stir and mix and knead and add more flour, until the dough, well... looks and feels about right.

And as I start listening to their stories again, I realize these ladies' "secret" to good noodles is the same as their "secret" for a good life: all it takes is some learning from experience. Then you start to know how to get it right. (November 15, 2001)

~♥~

Corn-fusion for the directionally challenged

Earlier this fall, my husband and two daughters wanted to spend a recent Sunday afternoon at a corn maze. It'll be fun, they assure me.

It'll be fun, they assure me.

I do not think this sounds like fun because I am, I openly admit, directionally-challenged. I once ordered a AAA Trip-Tik in order to make the journey from Dayton to Lexington, Kentucky.

"It'll be a good learning experience for the kids," my husband tells me, knowing I'm a sucker for learning experiences. "The challenge of a puzzle, using your wits..." So I decide to be a good sport and go with my family to the corn maze. I even leave behind the cell phone, the compass, and the backpack with flares and emergency provisions. After all, my husband *does* have a good sense of direction.

When we arrive at the local corn maze, my 9-year-old decides we should split up into teams. Her dad went with her younger sister, and she went with me.

Fortunately, my 9-year-old has inherited her dad's sense of direction. So I'm calm as we enter the maze and begin our quest: collect map pieces from mailboxes hidden in each of the 12 sections of the maze until we've put together the whole map. All is going well until my 9-year-old suddenly stops.

"What's the matter?" I ask.

"We're lost," she says, pointing at the mud puddle in which I'm standing. "That mud puddle. We've seen it before."

Apparently, in a maze, a sense of direction is only useful for helping you know when you're lost. As the adult in the situation, it's up to me to figure out how we can work our way through the maze.

Just as I'm about to ask her to climb up on my shoulders and scream for help, a pair of young boys come whizzing by, whooping and hollering. "We got lucky! We found the piece for section two!"

Blind luck! Now there's a plan! "Let's just keep walking until we find the mailbox for this section," I say. "How long can it take?"

Thirty-three minutes, as it turns out.

A young couple comes by, notes our discouraged expressions, and says, "If you're looking for the map piece for section three, it's right over there." And gives us directions. "That's cheating," my 9-year-old scowls.

"Uh, huh," I say. "Follow me." We get the next piece.

Now we've tried a sense of direction, blind luck, and cheating to get through the maze, none of which are particularly effective. Or satisfying.

I remember what my husband said. This is supposed to be a game, a puzzle in which you use your wits, right? Fine. If I'm going to freeze to death in the middle of a cornfield, I'm at least going to go down like a good parent and turn it into a life lesson.

Plus I'm out of ideas. So I say to my 9-year-old, "You like games. How do you go about winning games?"

She thinks for a minute. "How about—we use logic? We can use the map pieces we have to get to the bottom of the next section, then work our way to the top, always following along the right..."

That's just what we do. Eventually, after about two hours, we find our way through the maze with a completed map.

As we exit, I say to her, "Honey, you really learned something today. Life is just like a maze. You can try blind luck or cheating, but using your wits is really the best way to get through. Isn't that neat?"

And she looks up me and says, "Mom? Can we get hot chocolate?"

(December 2, 2001)

~ ♥ ~

Fair is fair when it comes to sport's trophy hair

The wigs are my 9-year-old daughter's idea.

She recently competed in a regional Taekwondo tournament in which she won two trophies: second place for "forms" (demonstrations of Taekwondo techniques) and third place in sparring.

Though pleased to have placed, she is dismayed that the figures on the trophies are... boys. So, she tells me a few evenings ago, we need to make wigs for her trophy-people. Now.

I'm not adept at wig making, so I try parental sleight-of-hand: pulling an explanation out of thin air and hoping she falls for it. "Maybe the person on the trophy is supposed to be either a girl or a boy."

"Mommmmm!" she wails, turning my one-syllable title into a multi-syllable lament that, to her pre-pre-teen view, I'm being clueless—again. "These are definitely *boys*. My sister's soccer trophies have *girls* with *ponytails*."

"There are," I inform her, "men who wear ponytails, so maybe your sister has a boy trophy with a ponytail and your trophies have girls with very, very short hair."

She flashes a look which clearly warns that if she has to say "Mommmmm" one more time, it will take at least 10 minutes and forevermore prove that I will *never* understand *anything about her.* This is not a fate I relish, and so I concede that she is right. Her trophies are bedecked with boys.

I try another approach. "I'm sure the boy trophies were just a matter of economics."

"Huh?"

"You were the only girl in your particular group for sparring, and only one of two for forms. Maybe the tournament organizers just wanted to save money by ordering boy trophies in bulk."

"Boys get boy trophies," she says matter-of-factly. "Girls should get girl trophies. Are you going to help me make wigs or not?"

I'm tempted to ask why she cares so much. After all, she won the darned trophies. Plus, hairstyles have never much interested her before. This is the same girl who was horrified at my glee in finding cute pony tail holders to match the color of her Taekwondo belt—and refused to wear them.

I'm tempted to tell her that she should feel blessed that no Taekwondo coach, competitor or referee has ever made her feel out of place for being interested in a sport that draws mostly males. That when I was her age, girls didn't play soccer, let alone one-on-one sports with boys. That her paternal grandmother could only play half-court basketball because full-court was considered too strenuous for girls—so she and her teammates once snuck into the school gym at night just for the thrill of playing full court. That for a long time, athletic girls were often considered... well... just a little odd.

But looking at my daughter, I realize telling her to accept "good enough" isn't... good enough. I realize she doesn't need a lesson in the long, challenging history of women's sports. Not just yet. Tonight, she needs wigs.

So we dig out some mauve yarn left over from a scouting project. Scissors. Tape.

We cut little strands of yarn and affix them to the tape. Then we stick the little mauve wigs on the heads of the Taekwondo trophies. Presto, chango. Girl trophies for a girl athlete.

And my 9-year-old smiles happily at them, all the way-too-early-pre-teen angst gone. There's a saying she is far too young to know about, or to yet understand: We've come a long way, baby. But with plucky 9-year-olds like her, we'll make the rest of the journey just fine.

(December 6, 2001)

~♥~

The tyranny of the empty cookie jar

'Twas the week before Christmas... nearly a whole year ago... when all through the house wafted the scent of cinnamon as my children and I baked snickerdoodle cookies. As we worked joyously, we sang *White Christmas* in three-part harmony, and snow fell prettily outside...

Uh, wait. The truth is, 'twas a week before Christmas about a year ago, and my daughters and I were baking snickerdoodles. The house smelled of cinnamon air freshener, which I'd sprayed to mask the odor of the burned first batch. My kids were helping with the second batch—some of the flour they flung at each other managed to get in the mixing bowl. Backstreet Boys played on the kids' CD player upstairs, while the downstairs radio blared "only seven shopping days till Christmas!" and the cat howled piteously at the door to get out. Even though it was sleeting.

I prefer to remember last year's cookie making as the first scenario. It's the only way I can explain how visions of cookies danced in my head and led me to ask my family for... a cookie jar.

I had this holiday-inspired notion that we should extend the fun of holiday cookie making to year-round. Sure, I occasionally make chocolate chip cookies—but that suddenly didn't seem good enough. We eat half the dough before it gets baked anyway.

So, imagine my delight last Christmas as I unwrapped a beautiful glass cookie jar. "So we can always see when you need to make more cookies," said older daughter--always the practical one.

"I wanted to get the one that looks like a pig and oinks when you open it," said younger daughter, such an imaginative child. "But Daddy said you wouldn't like that."

I looked at my husband, who wisely chose to say nothing, but smiled in a way that said everything: I'll still love you even when the cookie jar's empty.

Leftover Christmas cookies filled the jar through January.

In February, I bought Girl Scout cookies. Lots of them, reminding myself the purchase is for a good cause.

In March, we actually made chocolate-chip cookies.

In April, we got all the ingredients to make more chocolate chip cookies... and ate the chips on the way home from the grocery.

One afternoon in May, I came down with a severe case of guilt over not making cookies. So, I spread Nutella on saltines, and tried to pass these off as cookies to my kids.

In June, I bought three bags of Pepperidge Farm cookies. By the time I got home, two bags were left, and I emptied their contents into the cookie jar.

During July and August, the jar sat empty.

September saw a surge in cookie making. Chocolate chip! And more chocolate chip!

Halloween candy filled the jar in October. In November, I thought about making turkey-shaped sugar cookies, but just made a turkey instead.

Now, a full year later, 'tis a few weeks before Christmas. The cookie jar is empty. Rain falls outside. The cat howls; a Smash Mouth CD plays upstairs; the radio downstairs blares "only 14 shopping days until Christmas!" And my kids want to make cookies.

For just a moment, I'm struck by my year's worth of cookie-making failure. Then I realize my kids don't really care. They just want to make Christmas cookies with me. So I get out the flour and sugar, cinnamon and nutmeg... and the mop and the air freshener (just in case).

This year, I'm asking my family for stock in Pepperidge Farm.

(December 15, 2001)

~♥~

The perfect holiday stress reliever (for any time)
Every holiday season, in between shopping, wrapping, decorating, baking and celebrating, I hear and read all sorts of expert advice on how to cope with the stress of... shopping, wrapping, decorating, baking, celebrating...

As if I'm going to remember whether I'm supposed to inhale through my nose and exhale through my mouth, or vice-versa, as my kids holler on their way to the school bus, "we need three cans of food for the food drive... and a dozen cookies for the holiday party... *today*!"

Fortunately, I long ago devised a foolproof method for dealing with stress, whether holiday-induced or just-plain-year-round-life induced. Until now, I've only shared this secret technique with a few people, mostly because when I *have* shared it, I get looks that indicate I need more than just a little stress relief—perhaps a full month at a very private clinic.

Even so, in the holiday spirit of giving, I've decided I will share with you my absolutely foolproof method for coping with stress.

Shredding pantyhose.

I discovered this technique a few years ago when I came home from a lonnnnng day at work and discovered that I'd been walking around all day with one huge runner in my pantyhose. In a fit of frustration, I ripped that runner a bit longer... then kept going until my pantyhose were just a little palmful of nylon threads. By then, I felt so relaxed. I was even able to go into work the next day and refer to my boss by his actual name (rather than by all the names I'd hollered while shredding the pantyhose).

Since then, my pantyhose shredding has evolved. Shredding pantyhose you were going to throw away anyway because of a runner is fine for every-day stress—cat's hairball discovered in shoe, kid's gum stuck on carpet, etc., etc. But truly stressful events require *new* pantyhose to shred. Extremely stressful events require new and *expensive* pantyhose.

In fact, I once presented a beautifully gift-wrapped package to a friend who was going through a nasty divorce, telling her it contained the secret to stress-relief. She opened the box—and pulled out four packages of brand new pantyhose.

"What am I supposed to do," she sniffled. "Strangle him or hang myself?"

I explained my pantyhose-shredding-stress-relief theory. At first, she looked aghast. But then she started shredding—and by the time she was done with the first pair of pantyhose, they looked as though a mad dog had ripped into them. She, however, was grinning.

Pantyhose-shredding-as-stress-therapy works for a host of reasons. Compared to a month at a private clinic, it's cheap. It doesn't cause weight gain (all those cookies eaten in a fit of frustration over running out of tape half-way through gift-wrapping) or memory loss (all that eggnog to wash down the cookies). It doesn't result in having to later repair drywall or lamps, not to mention hurt feelings. It's simple to remember—you can inhale and exhale any old way you want while you shred pantyhose, even hold your breath if you want to. And pantyhose, at least for females, could well be the ultimate symbol for stress in general because—let's face it—even the nicest pantyhose are not very comfortable. (Men, feel free to shred your ties... or to buy your own pantyhose... whatever works.)

So this year, take a little tip from me. Spend a few minutes away from shopping, wrapping, decorating, baking, and celebrating to stock up on pantyhose. For shredding. The perfect holiday (and year-round) stress-reliever. (December 20, 2001)

~♥~

Pageant is perfect, flaws and all

My 9-year-old daughter wants to wear her oversized snake T-shirt from the natural history museum as her costume in the Christmas pageant. She's part of the ensemble that's to open the pageant: girls at a slumber party introducing the Christmas story to a girl who hasn't heard it.

My 8-year-old daughter, a.k.a. Shepherd No. Four, keeps saying her two lines as one long word. With her eyes squeezed tightly shut.

I try explaining to my 9-year-old why a snake T-shirt as a pajama top is fine at home but probably not the best costume choice for a Christmas pageant.

"Remember the snake's role in the story of Adam and Eve?" I say. "We'll just go shopping and get you a nice pajama set, maybe something pink, silky..."

"But, mommmmm," she wails, "I *have* to wear this T-shirt because it's my *only comfortable* night clothes and I won't be able to act if I'm not comfortable..."

I turn my attention back to my 8-year-old. "Dear, you might try saying each word one at a time. And opening your eyes while you speak."

"But, mommmmm," she wails, "I can *see* my lines with my eyes closed, so it's more like reading..."

It's easy for parents to miss the point of the annual Christmas pageant. After all, the story is so well known that it's easier to focus on more immediate concerns—the creative, new ways in which ones children can be embarrassing.

Finally, it's time for the Christmas pageant. And I realize I'm not the only parent just a wee bit nervous. I know this, because along with our holiday outfits, we're all wearing smiles stretched just a bit too thin.

The story begins. Oldest daughter, as part of the slumber-party-intro-ensemble, appears wearing not new silky pajamas, but a different oversized T-shirt (this one from a summer camp) and pajama bottoms—a last minute compromise.

Mary and Joseph appear, discuss their situation with Angels No. 1 and 2, then take off on their trek to Bethlehem in their Reeboks and robes. After being booted out by a gleeful innkeeper (played by a young actor who intuitively understands that the villainous roles are always the most fun), they take up residence in a stable (a.k.a. a decorated refrigerator box, held up by the Patron Saint of Christmas Pageants, who has dominion over gravity).

Shepherds 1 through 6 arrive herding two sheep, but somehow the youngest sheep makes a break for it and toddles off to find her mother. Shepherd No. 4 keeps her eyes open and says her lines as if they are *two* words. I consider this success and relax a little.

Two wise women and one wise man appear and, drawing upon their collective 12 years' life experience, deliver their lines most sagely but are unable to offer wisdom to help the shepherds retrieve their wandering sheep (now with mom). Gifts are presented to the baby in the manger... and suddenly—too suddenly, it seems—the pageant is over.

All of us, young and old and somewhere in-between, grandparents and parents and children, sing *Joy to the World*. As we do, a little girl, too young to be in the pageant, breaks forth from the pews, toddles forward, and starts dancing.

No one stops her as we sing. I'm glad, and looking around, I can see the other grownups are glad, too, for her dance serves as the perfect summary of what the children's annual reenactment of the Christmas story is really all about anyway: not perfection, but pirouettes of joy, bounds of grace, and leaps of faith.

(December 27, 2001)

~♥~

Rivalry takes a holiday

When my 8-year-old tells me she wants to dress for her older sister's basketball practices, I figure she has just one motivation: she wants to get away with wearing shorts in winter.

My eight-year-old assures me she has a much better reason. "There might be a practice game," she says. "And they might need someone to help!" I do so adore the optimism of 8-year-olds.

My 10-year-old, however, seriously doubts the purity of her little sister's motives. "She just wants to do whatever I do! She's always following me around!"

My daughters were born 21 months, 2 weeks, 5 days, 18 hours and 2 minutes apart. So, in many cases, it is reasonable for them to share friends and activities. However, I think they could have been born just 2 seconds apart, and big sis would have crawled out of the womb whining that little sis is "always following her around."

I've long given up on trying to tell older daughter that her little sis just admires her, or tell younger daughter that big sis needs time to herself. Explanations don't work with kids. I have instead developed a favorite technique for Parental Management of Sibling Rivalry that works at least half the time, entitled: "I AM The Enemy Which My Daughters Share In Common."

In this case, I employ the technique by instructing both daughters to dress for basketball practice in shorts—with sweatpants over top for the ride to the gym. As they troop off to get dressed, they grouse about my dorky fashion sense and my ridiculous belief that 20-degree weather is too cold for shorts. I consider this a victory for Parental Management of Sibling Rivalry. After all, they're grousing together.

Every week, my 8-year-old dresses for her big sister's basketball practices. She watches her big sis practice, longing in her eyes. She wants to be out there, too, and my explaining that she's just a year too young for rec league basketball in our town doesn't help. My 10-year-old pointedly ignores her at practice, but at home practices shooting hoops in the driveway with her.

And then, finally, glorious opportunity: coach calls a scrimmage game at practice. Since the team has eight girls, he'll let my 8-year-old and another player's big sister participate, so they can have two sides of five players. The youngest is ecstatic! She trots out onto the gym floor right over to her sister, eager for instruction. Big sister, of course, rolls eyes and moves away.

The scrimmage game ensues, with my daughters playing on the same side. And then, the most miraculous thing occurs. My 10-year-old actually passes the ball to my 8-year-old, who is so excited that she forgets to dribble as she takes the ball down court. All the girls are hollering that this is traveling, a definite no-no in basketball. Except, I note in amazement, my 10-year-old. She is grinning. Proudly. Hey, at least little sis caught the ball. At least she gets the concept. And now... little sis is six feet away from the basket... and taking a shot... and the ball goes in!

Big sis runs over to little sis and catches her up in a hug that's all pride over her little sister's first-ever basketball game basket. Never mind that the basket doesn't count. Sibling rivalry is momentarily forgotten in a pure moment of sibling pride.

It's a precious, rare moment that I cherish.

Especially a few minutes after practice ends, when we're back in the car, and these two sisters who really do admire each other are in the backseat... fighting over leftover French fries.

(February 11, 2002)

~♥~

Sweetie, is that wall half empty? Or half full?

After years of trying to keep straight whether it's me or my husband who is supposed to be from Mars, Venus or a fifth moon twice removed from some planet in a galaxy far, far away, I have finally figured out one of the main differences between men and women.

Men look at a blank wall and see a wall.

Women look at a blank wall and see opportunity.

Understanding this difference has taken me 18-plus years and living in five homes in three states.

I say: Stencils! Wallpaper! Wall borders! Paint with names like Lemongrass and Vacillating Violet! Pictures! Plaques!

He says: Off-white drywall.

Recently, I point to an unadorned wall and say "Look, sweetie! The perfect spot for that lovely little tapestry I just bought!"

The pathetically bare expanse of wall happens to be in our home's entryway, which happens to have high ceilings, so hanging that lovely little tapestry will require someone getting out a ladder. I am afraid of heights. This is why I feel compelled to point out the need to hang the tapestry to my husband while calling him sweetie.

My sweetie moans. "But that's the last blank wall in our house! Look at it. Isn't it great just the way it is?" He gazes up at the wall with dewy-eyed admiration that is usually only reserved for something he finds particularly moving—like his favorite football team winning in overtime. "Drywall," he says. "Off-white drywall..."

I'm starting to wonder whether a man really painted the Sistine Chapel. A sis, Michelle-angelo perhaps, seems more likely; it's hard to imagine a man actually applying more than one color to a wall.

"The wall needs something to add zip," I say. "Besides, I gave in on the window toppers, didn't I?"

For years, I have contended that all windows need window toppers. My husband swears windows just need mini-blinds. I say that windows without window toppers look naked. He says that window toppers do not serve any actual function and are therefore a waste of perfectly blank drywall.

We now have window toppers in just about every room in the house—with the exception of the living room. And it's an exception that nags at me, which occasionally makes me nag at him.

"Bringing up the window toppers isn't fair," he says. "I was willing to compromise."

This is, in fact, technically true. The last time I whined about the living room windows needing decoration, he offered to make window toppers. Out of chrome.

Chrome window toppers over the living room window, he said, would serve as a reflective surface for the light coming in the opposite dining room window, thus increasing the ambient lighting and adding a touch of solar heat. Decorative *and* functional. I think he was kidding. At least, I tell myself he was kidding. But now, I think, maybe not.

"Tell you what. I was only going to get this one tapestry," I say. "But don't you think seasonal tapestries would be nice? Tulips in the spring, pumpkins in the fall. If you don't mind that, then I'll be glad to agree to those chrome window toppers you've been wanting."

He goes a bit pale. "Let's just skip the chrome window toppers," he says, "and stick to the one tapestry, OK?"

And with that my very own Michelangelo-esque sweetie trots out to the garage to retrieve the ladder.

After 18-plus years of marriage and five homes in three states, we may not have figured out the art of decorating... but we're starting to figure out the art of compromise.
(February 18, 2002)

~ ♥ ~

CHAPTER 2

~❤~

The Ups and Downs of Family Life... a.k.a. Stairway Roller Coaster

Nothin' wrong with just foolin'
The last thing we parents want our kids to see us as is foolish.

After all, the dictionary definition of a fool is "a person lacking in judgment or prudence." And parenting is one job that demands applying constant, vigilant good judgment. No matter how much our kids swear they-hate-us-and-will-never-talk-to-us-when-we're-old because we refuse to give in on choco-bombs cereal for dinner, or on wearing flip-flops to softball practice, or whatever else our kids come up with that clearly shows a definite lack of judgment.

On a recent rainy Saturday afternoon, my kids told me they were bored. I gave my standard reply to such pleas: "There's plenty to do. Let's start with cleaning your rooms, feeding the cats, sweeping the bathrooms..."

"But mommmmm," they whined. "We want something fun to do."

I considered their case and applied good judgment. After all, they'd had a long school week and needed a break. So with the wisdom of Solomon and a regal wave of my hand, I said, "Be gone. Use your imaginations to come up with something unique to entertain yourselves."

They looked at each other. They smiled and ran from the room. My good judgment inspired me to think: Uh oh.

Ten minutes later, I heard a thumpety-thump-thump and simultaneous giggling. Again—thumpety-thump-thump... giggle, giggle.

As every parent knows, the only thing scarier than two siblings fighting is two siblings getting along. While giggling.

So, I went to investigate—and caught them in the act of riding in plastic trash bags down the stairs.

Being a parent of good judgment, I of course sternly told them that their "stairway roller coaster—" their term, not mine—was not safe. They could put an eye out! Wear out the stair carpeting! Flatten a cat!

But that evening, after the kids went to bed, I couldn't help thinking about how giddy they'd seemed while thumpety-thumping along on their stairway roller coaster. How disappointed they'd been when I took their plastic bags away. How they'd spent the rest of the day alternating between squabbling and whining to watch TV.

Maybe I hadn't used such good judgment. Maybe I needed to investigate a little further, just to be sure I'd really made the right judgment... I dug out a plastic trash bag. I hopped in and sat down on the top stair, took a deep breath—and launched myself.

Thumpety-thump-thump. At the bottom of the stairs, I hopped up, about to race back up for just one more ride, when suddenly, the light at the top of the stairs came on.

I turned around slowly. There they were—my two daughters. Staring at me.

"You could put an eye out," said the 10-year-old.

"Do you know how much it costs to replace carpeting?" said the 8-year-old.

I had no choice. I had to apply good judgment. "Go get your own bags if you want to play," I said.

Solomon might've been proud. If they'd only had trash bags back in his day.

(April 1, 2002)

~♥~

A "life-changing" farm tour

Looking back, I'm not sure what compelled me to take our Girl Scout troop to visit a farm. My idealistic vision—blurry now—was that we'd cast aside our cushy suburban-hood to experience a real, working farm.

So a few weeks later, I'm in a barn at a local demonstration farm with 10 Girl Scouts. I feel a tug and turn to see a blue-eyed Scout staring up at me. "It stinks in here," she says.

As her leader, I feel obliged to impart some, well, leader-like wisdom. So I say, "Now, dear, we're here to broaden our horizons. This could be a life-changing experience."

Then our guide describes the roles pigs play in our lives, while pointing to two very large pigs who are staring at us. These roles seem to be: bacon, pork chops, ham and pig's ear doggie treats.

I feel another tug and this time turn to see a brown-eyed Scout staring up at me. "I don't really like knowing where my meat comes from."

"We must keep an open mind, dear," I say. "This could be a life-changing experience."

We go to the next stall, where I see a small, grayish animal. I ask, "Is this a mule or donkey?"

The guide kindly smiles at me. "It's a calf," she says. I stare at her. "You know, a baby cow."

I do know cows. I've seen pictures of them. I've even driven past fields in which they've been wandering. Cows are supposed to be tan or white with black spots. Not gray. Mules and donkeys are gray. Maybe, I think, this animal is some kind of cow-mule-donkey-mutant. Before I can suggest this possibility, however, our guide tells us we're going to leave the barn to go see other cows out in the pasture.

Several Scouts are now blue from breath-holding, while a few others are green from not breath-holding, so I agree that going outside for fresh air in the cow pasture is a good idea.

That's when I feel the next tug. I turn around and look down into the gray eyes of... the cow-mule-donkey-mutant. It is eating my shirt, starting with the hem and working quickly up to my collar. I wonder if perhaps this animal is also part goat. I jerk most of my shirt from the cow-mule-donkey-goat's teeth and hurry out to the cow pasture.

There, I discover two things: "Fresh air" and "cow pasture" do not belong in the same sentence; and there are 10 cows, all lolling about on the ground, and all of them are some variation of beige—bisque, ecru, taupe. Not a single gray cow!

Just as I'm about to point this out to the guide, she informs us that these cows are all pregnant.

I'm not sure how you tell a pregnant cow from a non-pregnant cow, but this new information makes me nervous.

What if the cows have a collective hormonal surge, pin us down, and demand something yummy to eat—now? What would a pregnant cow crave, anyway? I craved milkshakes and hamburgers when I was pregnant... but somehow I don't think this will satisfy a herd of hormonally crazed cows.

The rest of the tour (something about sheep... chickens...) is a blur. My next clear memory is sheer relief at seeing a sure sign of suburban civilization: a McDonald's. After returning the Girl Scouts safely to their parents, I pull up to the drive-through and start to order my usual stress-relieving snack—a double-cheeseburger.

But our trip turned to the farm turns out to be life-changing for me after all.

I get a McSalad instead.

(April 8, 2002)

~♥~

Trees: a very good policy
Two trees are leafing out in my back yard. And, my insurance agent tells me, it's time for an annual review of my life insurance policy.

Looked at separately, neither fact seems particularly remarkable. But thanks to a twist of circumstances two springs ago, my back yard trees and my insurance policy are forever linked in my mind. Together, they give me an annual object lesson on how to balance the pragmatic—and the soulful—in life.

Two springs ago, I'd been in business for myself for a whopping six months—long enough to appreciate self-employment's upsides (cat-on-lap while working, personalized coffee choices) and recognize a few downsides, one of which is the necessity of buying your own life insurance.

Two springs ago, we'd been in our new house for a whopping nine months—long enough to appreciate its upsides (roominess, great neighbors) and recognize a few downsides, the largest of which was an absolutely tree-less back yard.

I love trees. At our previous home, we had a line of trees along our property line that I adored so much that when a certain tree cutting contractor of a certain utility company came along with a piece of paper that said his company was authorized to cut down the trees, I threatened to chain myself to a tree and call a certain local television station. I was seven months pregnant at the time. The tree-cutting contractor was smart enough to know a hormonally crazed woman when he saw one, so he just trimmed the tops of the trees.

Two kids later, though, we outgrew our tiny starter home. The roomier home we fell in love with happened to be built on a lot that was once part of a cornfield. Hence, our new back yard featured a lot of thistles. But no trees.

So one day two springs ago, I found and fell in love with two trees (one birch, one maple) and put them on hold at a local nursery. I wanted them for me. But I also wanted them for my kids. I liked the idea of shady back yard trees under which my kids could eat popsicles on a hot summer day. Or use as a base for "tag." Or flop down under to stare up through the leaves at a starry night.

Later that day, my agent came by to discuss life insurance. To tell the truth, I was so excited about finding the two perfect trees that I'd forgotten about our appointment.

As I settled down at the kitchen table to discuss insurance, I told myself I needed to think frugally. I really should invest in only one or the other—insurance. Or trees. And, of course, I told myself, insurance would be the most pragmatic choice.

Now, it's a strange thing on a warm spring afternoon to listen to your insurance agent describe how important a life insurance policy would be to your family should you, well, die... while at the same time glancing out the window at your children playing in a sunny (but treeless) back yard. And that's when it struck me.

Sometimes in life we need policies... for insurance.

Sometimes in life we need trees... for assurance.

So I did the only thing I really could do. I got both. And every spring, when our back yard trees leaf out and my insurance agent comes by for a review meeting... I'm glad I did.

(April 22, 2002)

~ ♥ ~

Sibling rivalry strikes out

Until this past Mother's Day, I had the perfect response when one or the other of my daughters proclaimed, regarding her sister, "You love her more!"

I'd just look in the brown-or-blue eyes of whichever daughter was making this outrageous claim, and say, "Now, darling, you know I'd throw myself in front of a train to save either of you."

This was the perfect response for three reasons: 1.) It's true; 2.) It inspires blue-or-brown eyed daughter to say, "But Mom, I don't want you to do that!" and thus ends the conversation; 3.) We don't live near any train tracks.

Then along came spring softball, which both my kids elected to play. And for which, due to age differences, they were assigned different teams. Upon crosschecking team schedules, I was thrilled to see no overlaps, except just one... for Sunday before last. The only game for the entire season when both kids' games started at the exact same time. One o'clock. On Mother's Day.

My kids were on this one like sharks in a feeding frenzy—only it was me they circled, baring their little teeth as they took turns saying, "She'll go to my game on Mommy's day, 'cause she loves me more!"

Now, I suppose if I had any sense, I'd have told my husband to take the sharkettes to their games, while I went out for a movie, or a manicure, or both. It was Mom's day, right? But the truth is, I really wanted to be at both games. I didn't want to choose. Suddenly, I wished we did live along the tracks. First I prayed for rain. Then—knowing that the Almighty really wasn't likely to adjust the forces of nature to fit my personal needs—I started plotting and planning.

So it was that on Mother's Day, on the way to the ball field, I found myself explaining the following plan to my husband as he drove.

"OK, listen closely. Blue eyes has her game in field A, whereas brown eyes has her game in field C. We'll meet at the port-o-potty by field B every ten minutes. Do you have your nose clip?"

"Sure," said hubby, gripping the wheel.

"We each have 27 seconds to summarize what's happened at the game we've just come from. That gives us each three seconds to cross to the other field. You're wearing good running shoes, right?"

"Right-y-o," said hubby, staring straight ahead.

"And you have your cell phone charged up, right? We'll just have to call each other if anything really spectacular happens at the game we're watching. Now, as for videotaping..."

A kid piped up from the back seat. "Uh, Mom? Whose game are you going to go to first?"

Silence. I consider. Finally I say, with great mom-authority-bravado, "No problem! We'll just flip a coin!"

"I get to be heads."

"That's not fair! You're always heads."

"Nuh-uh. Mom always lets you be heads."

"Nuh-uh. Mom always lets you be heads."

And at that exact moment—I jest not—thunder roared. Lightening struck. The heavens opened, and a great deluge came down. And down. And down some more. The baseball games were rained out. Sometimes, a mother's prayers are answered.

(May 20, 2002)

~♥~

Embracing Memorial Day

Officially, Memorial Day is set aside for remembering those who have died in our nation's service.

Unofficially, Memorial Day is also when we celebrate the sweet start of summer. Pools open. Picnics abound.

As a kid, Memorial Day meant a trip to visit family graves because, like most families, we stretched the official purpose of Memorial Day to include remembering all loved ones who had died.

But the holiday also meant that the glorious barefoot, Popsicle, bike-riding days of summer were just a calendar-page flip away. Staying somber on graveyard visits was a challenge—especially when I was itching to kick off my shoes and run around.

So, I've never been comfortable with this holiday's mix of solemnity and glee... until this Memorial Day. Although she doesn't realize it, I have my Great Aunt Cassie to thank for my ability to finally manage this holiday's emotional balancing act.

At 93 years old, Great Aunt Cassie lives by herself—her husband passed away several years ago—in the same small Kentucky town in which she grew up. She doesn't come close to breaking the 5-foot mark, but when her neighbors fuss at her for still tending a large vegetable garden, she stands tall and reminds them she's been gardening for eight-plus decades, and isn't about to stop. Since Great Aunt Cassie doesn't drive a car—in fact, she never has—she walks to church and the corner store.

I, on the other hand, am lucky if I can coax a petunia to survive in a window box until July Fourth. And I spend so much time driving around that our car payment would be more appropriately called "rent."

But on my last visit to her house, I discovered my Great Aunt Cassie and I have more in common than I realized. As we watched my kids play with a toy that once belonged to Great Aunt Cassie's daughter—who now has two grown children of her own—we talked about the joys of children. And then to my surprise, my always upbeat Great Aunt Cassie started crying. She had, she said, lost a child once.

First, I was amazed that she could still feel 60-year-old grief so freshly. Then—before I could push it away—my own grief welled, as I realized that I was about the same age she'd been when I, too, had lost a child.

I'd grieved at the time—then sealed away the ache in a memory vault. In this age of "been there, done that," we tell ourselves not to dwell too long on anything, including grieving. Somehow—even if no one else directly tells us— we tell ourselves that we must quickly move on past losses.

Now, I don't have anything approximating the wisdom of my Great Aunt Cassie. But I do have enough sense to recognize that you don't get to be a happy, independent, beloved 93-year-old without figuring something out about dealing with life... and its losses. So, finally, I took the only sensible course of action. I joined my Great Aunt Cassie in a good old-fashioned cry.

Then we took a good look at our kids—mine still playing on the family room floor, hers cooking up lunch in the kitchen. And we went right back to rejoicing in the blessings we each have.

This Memorial Day, I'm going to remember my Great Aunt Cassie's wisdom. Let tears fall, if they must. Let laughter billow, when it can.

(May 27, 2002)

~ ♥ ~

Dads don't baby-sit

My husband does not baby-sit.

Not only does he not run a business watching other people's kids for an hourly fee, he does not baby-sit our kids, either.

This fact shocks some people. Every now and then I have reason to be away from my home, without husband or kids, in the evenings. And every now and then, while I am out on these no-husband-or-kids-in-tow-occasions, someone will say to me, "Is your husband baby-sitting the kids?"

That's when I say, "No, my husband doesn't baby-sit."

And then, as the inquirer looks stunned, I drop the real shocker. "My husband is, however, home with our children."

You see, while he won't baby-sit, he is more than glad to parent.

I've checked with my husband, and in our 10 years of being parents, during which time he has on more than a few occasions ventured out without wife or kids in tow, no one has ever asked him, "Where are your kids? Is your wife baby-sitting them?"

Somehow, to some folks, even after years of equal-rights struggling, moms parent—but dads just baby-sit. And I must admit, I can understand the temptation of thinking that way.

Several weeks after we had our first child, my husband said to me, "You need some time to write. I'll take care of the baby if she wakes up." I eagerly went to my office to work for the first time since we'd brought home Baby No. 1.

Three minutes into my working session—just long enough to vaguely recall the difference between a noun and a verb—baby started screaming. My first thought was to go "rescue" both baby and Dad. But something told me not to. I reminded myself that my husband is a perfectly competent human being. If our baby needed changed or comforted or fed, he was as capable as I of taking care of her needs.

I didn't go back to writing, though. Instead, I closed my eyes and simply sat, focusing on my breathing—in, out; whoo, whee; pant, pant, pant. (Lamaze training was finally useful.) Yes, Daddy eventually took care of whatever need our baby had. She eventually stopped wailing. I eventually wandered out of my office and found husband/dad/competent-human-being watching a football game, with baby blissfully asleep on his chest.

"Good writing session?" he asked.

"Great, thanks," I said.

I'd like to say that ever since then I haven't been tempted to fall prey to the dads-just-baby-sit mentality. But I find I have to be ever vigilant against doing so, because there's plenty of pressure to give in to such prejudiced thinking.

It's the fact that in every public place I know—stores, restaurants, and so on—the women's rooms often have diaper-changing tables, while the men's rooms only occasionally do.

It's television ads, like the recent one for a certain department store, in which the mom is out shopping alone, and the kids are destroying the house while the poor, bewildered, obviously incompetent dad says, "Where's your mom?" The ad closes with a tag line, "Don't worry Dad. The sale will be over soon."

I'd like to propose a different tag line. Real parents—both moms and dads—don't baby-sit. They just do their best, one day at a time.

(June 17, 2002)

~♥~

A double scoop of understanding

It's one of those rare times when I have a chance to focus on just the 8-year-old, because the 10-year-old is at summer camp for a whole week.

So we make plans. Seeing movies that the 10-year-old would hate (anything even hinting at ghosts, such as Scooby Doo) and the 8-year-old would love. Lunch at the 8-year-old's favorite restaurant—which, of course, the 10-year-old declares "gross." Swimming—lots and lots of swimming. Friends over—without the 10-year-old and her friends' eye rolling at the childish ways of 8-year-olds.

Of course, the flip side of getting spoiled as a temporarily-only-child is also getting all the not-so-fun attention.

That's because for a parent the flip side of doting on said temporarily-only-child is focusing on not-so-great habits that, in the shuffle of dealing with multiple kids, tend to get overlooked.

I should know better, but I decide that while of course my temporarily-only-child-who-is-8 and I will do fun stuff, I will also take the one-on-one time as a chance to help her with a little self-improvement, specifically in how she dresses herself.

Yes, the 8-year-old has clothes. Lots of them. Nice ones, which she picked out on shopping trips that she very much enjoyed.

So when, near the end of third grade, she suddenly started wanting to wear only T-shirts and jeans (or shorts), I was surprised. When she started trying to wear the same T-shirt every day, I was bewildered. When she tried to go to school wearing one of her sister's T-shirts—which she'd fished out of the dirty clothes because, as she explained, "the older the T-shirt, the better"—I stopped trying to figure out her behavior and instituted a new rule: each new day, a fresh T-shirt.

At least that got her back to wearing clean T-shirts, but she still prefers old ones—a fact that bugs me, considering all the nice (non-T-shirt) clothes she has.

So on our first mom-spoils-the-8-year-old-outing to an ice cream parlor, I bring up the subject.

"I see you're wearing an old T-shirt again," I say.

She stares at me warily over the top of her chocolate double-dip cone.

"And I think it's time we talked about that," I go on.

She gives me a look that threatens to curdle her—and everyone else's—ice cream.

"Mom, I just like wearing comfy T-shirts, OK?"

I have a sinking feeling that, instead of spoiling the 8-year-old, I'm about to spoil our outing. But I'm the mom, right? I know best, right? So I start to plunge on with a lecture about how I'd like her to wear her nicer clothes more often, when a mom and her teenage daughter (dressed very nicely in non-T-shirt apparel) walk past. They are laughing, having a good time.

But then the teenage daughter sees some friends. And she turns to her mom and says, "You're not going to stay in here while I talk to them, are you?"

And the mom—with a sigh of resignation—goes outside alone to eat her ice cream cone, while her teen daughter stays inside to laugh, instead, with her friends.

At this point, my 8-year-old daughter looks at me and says, "What, mom?"

And I look back at her and say, "You know what? I like your T-shirt. How's your ice-cream?"

She grins with relief—and so do I.

She'll stop wearing T-shirts all the time soon enough. (July 29, 2002)

~♥~

What I learned on my (spontaneous) summer vacation
As I lugged a six-pound stack of maps, travel brochures, guidebooks, and travel magazines into the family room, my husband suggested that this year's family vacation should be spontaneous. A grand family experiment, he said. I dropped my load of travel data to the floor.

"Spon—spontaneous?" I stuttered. "As in no schedules?"

"How about side trips?" our 10-year-old asked. "Some families take cool side trips. They see caves and weird things in jars in museums. I could put it in my school report this fall—what I learned on my summer vacation..."

"Side trips?" I squeaked. "Unplanned?"

My husband grinned. "And no reservations."

When I came to, my family fanned me with maps.

"When's the last time you were spontaneous?" my husband wanted to know.

"I had rocky road ice cream once. Instead of pistachio."

"That was 1992."

That was also before having kids. Spontaneous ended when I became pregnant and had to start taking regularly scheduled mega-vitamins. Motherhood has only confirmed my calendar-consulting, list-making tendency.

I keep checklists of my to-do lists, which are categorized by activity type, cross-indexed on a spreadsheet and backed up on computer diskette. I long ago reached the point where I'd rather lose my checkbook than my daytimer. And when it comes to travelling, I ordered a AAA Trip-tik for our first family trip outside of Dayton, Ohio—to the Cincinnati Zoo.

"Does spontaneous mean we can stop for ice cream, even if it's not part of the plan?" my 8-year-old asked, wistfully.

That did it. Eight-year-olds should not think in terms of planning when it comes to ice cream. So I said, "Yes, that's just what spontaneous means. And that's just what we're doing this vacation. No schedules. No pre-planned activities."

My kids started dancing in circles. I looked at my husband. "And no reservations." He nearly fell over.

A month later, we were set to go. We did have an end destination—Florida—but no reservations or plans about what we'd do on our way to Florida, or on the way back. I'd been brave until the moment of departure.

After our first spontaneous vacation act—stopping for a pizza dinner—I quit worrying that we'd starve to death because we hadn't planned out all our meal stops. Then, after we spontaneously let the kids pick the motel for the night (a Kastle Inn, which they liked because of the name), I stopped thinking we'd have to sleep in our car. The next day, when we spontaneously stopped at Cumberland Falls in Kentucky and not only viewed the waterfall, but took a spontaneous raft right up to it, I stopped worrying we'd never get to do anything fun, since we hadn't researched and scheduled activities.

There were plenty of other spontaneous moments. Getting lost in Tampa because we weren't properly equipped with maps wasn't so fun. But most of the spontaneous things were fun. Like stopping in Georgia at Edmund Brothers Pecans and sitting under the 83 year-old pecan trees and eating ice cream just because our 8-year-old wanted to.

So, what did I learn on my summer vacation?

Spontaneity is a worthy part of any good plan.

(August 26, 2002)

~♥~

Coloring outside the lines

When I was a kid, I loved school-supply shopping. So now, school-supply shopping with my own kids is not a chore—it's a ritual: I take one kid at a time to shop for her supplies. Afterward, we celebrate with ice cream or some other treat.

Ah, the joy of as-yet unmarred paper and folders! New glue sticks and scissors! The fresh smell of a new box of crayons!

Hokey? Maybe. We don't care. We just revel in our annual school-supply shopping ritual.

But, alas, this year the ritual for my soon-to-be-fifth-grader is nearly ruined. She carefully selects fresh, new pencils. Glue sticks. Notebooks and folders. But then her eyes widen with horror.

"There are no... no crayons on the list!" She wails in the middle of the discount store.

I understand her dismay. Crossing the line from needing-crayons to not-needing-crayons means you're one step farther away from childhood, and one step closer to adolescence.

Ah, the challenges of being 10.

And I share my daughter's alarm. For one thing, I'm not quite ready to relinquish her to the journey-to-adolescence. And for another, it strikes me that it's been a very, very long time since I've had crayons, too. Suddenly, I miss them. Which may sound silly, but think about it—

wasn't coloring one of the most comforting, relaxing things you ever did as a kid?

But I'm too old for crayons, I tell myself, so I cast about in my mind for the next best thing—maybe a new lipstick. Perhaps something in Plum Passion will put a little zip in my autumn.

Ah, the challenges of being 40-something.

I ask my daughter if she minds if we stop by the health and beauty department. She gives me a long look. We never mix school-supply shopping with other shopping, her look says. But she shrugs, and we head off in that direction.

As I contemplate the virtues of Plum Passion versus Radiant Red, my soon-to-be-fifth-grader speaks up.

"Mom, I'm old enough to wear lipstick to school now," she declares.

What? This is the same kid who moments ago was mourning the absence of crayons from her school-supply list?

"I don't think so," I snap, suddenly more sure than ever that I'm not ready for this kid's journey-to-adolescence. I'm suddenly not interested in lipstick (was I ever, really?), either.

"Fine," she says. "I'll make my own. I'll just use Chapstick and... and crayon shavings!"

I'm about to point out that this might prove problematic, given that crayons weren't on her shopping list. But it doesn't seem right to use sarcasm in this moment with my daughter, who's torn between wanting crayons and wanting to wear lipstick, who's looking at me with both defiance and vulnerability.

Instead, I confess that deep down I miss crayons, too. That every now and then, I'd rather be coloring on paper than on my face.

We strike a deal. We'll get the Plum Passion lipstick for me, but she can borrow it to wear around the house. And we'll go back and get a box of stay-at-home crayons for her, but I can borrow them every now and again.

After all, whether you're 10 or 40-something, you're going to keep aging. You might as well do it colorfully. (September 2, 2002)

~♥~

OJ options create big squeeze

These days, it's easier for me to select a bottle of wine than a jug of orange juice—and I don't know a thing about wine.

I used to know about orange juice. People in Florida grew oranges, squeezed juice, and shipped it off for the rest of us to buy. I could run into the grocery store, grab a jug of orange juice, and check out in three minutes flat.

Now people in Florida grow oranges, squeeze juice, and start messing with it. A few days ago I went to the grocery with a foot long list. I spent an hour at the grocery store—30 minutes buying enough provisions to get two adults, two kids, three cats and one very nervous fish through one week of life with no shortages. I spent the remaining 30 minutes trying to find the right orange juice.

What happened? One minute, there are two choices for orange juice: frozen or in a jug. Now, there are so many varieties I need a spreadsheet to keep up: no pulp, some pulp, medium pulp, high pulp. Calcium added. Original. Homestyle. Mixed with strawberry, or pineapple, or banana juice. Even mixed with tangerine juice—which, frankly, raises the question: how can you tell?

I admit I was glad when orange-juice-with-calcium first came out. A great way to get more calcium into the family's diet, right?

But then everyone caught on to the fact that there are all these choices, and orange juice shopping suddenly became complex.

I need no pulp, calcium for the 10-year-old... but high pulp if she's having an overnight because that's all her best friend will drink. The 9-year-old thinks if calcium can be added to orange juice, then Vitamin C should be added to chocolate milk, so she can forego orange juice entirely, but she's willing to consume the orange/strawberry juice (some pulp) version.

And so, I find myself standing, trance-like, before the orange juice case, my brain turning to, well, pulp, as all thoughts about anything else are blocked out by a hurricane of orange juice questions.

For example, am I really making the right orange juice choice? I thought I was being health-conscious just by getting calcium added juice. But look... another variety has cropped up! Double C with 100-percent E! And A, C, and E with Calcium! And C & E plus Zinc! Would one of those be better? Or should I buy some of each and make my own orange juice concoction?

And somehow, all these choices—while overwhelming—make me wonder about the choices I don't have. For example, I can get orange/pineapple/banana juice. Or orange/pineapple juice. But not orange/banana juice. Why not? Is it because some marketing focus group said OK to mixing up just pineapples and oranges but not to bananas and oranges? Is a pineapple lobby shutting out bananas from having exclusive rights to mixing with oranges? Am I just waaaaay out of the mainstream if I really want orange-banana juice with no pineapples squeezing in, and if so, I worry, what does this say about me?

And with all these combinations and options, what's next? Orange juice merlot (no pulp)? Orange-pineapple-cranberry chardonnay (with vitamins A through K)? Where will it all end?

It's almost enough to make me stalk off without any juice at all and just go get... a plain orange that I can squeeze myself.

(December 2, 2002)

~♥~

CHAPTER 3

~❤~

My Houseplants Have Fleas

Unexpected gift: lessons from Santa's candy book

Every year—somewhere around August, when I'm longing for cooler temperatures while the stores are displaying winter coats—I promise myself that I will not torture myself over *this* year's Christmas shopping.

I promise myself that I will not make myself crazy, scurrying around on multiple shopping trips motivated by the fear that I have not gotten exactly the right things, or enough things, or the perfect things.

Somehow, though, I never quite manage to keep that promise to myself when Christmas comes around. So, of course, a few days ago I found myself out on yet another holiday shopping errand, fretting over what I had bought, what I hadn't bought, and what I was about to buy.

Then I saw it... the perfect Christmas gift... Santa's Candy Book. No, not a tome authored by Mr. Claus regarding the history of candy canes. One of those little boxes, designed to look and open up like a book, filled with eight or so rolls of hard candy.

The sight of it made me put down all the other stuff I was holding, and pick up the "candy book."

Suddenly I was 9-years-old again, and wrapping up a "candy book" as the perfect gift for a special recipient— my bus driver. When I got on the bus, and gave the gift to him, he didn't worry about keeping to an exact schedule. He opened it right then and there. And, as I watched breathlessly, he reacted with great surprise and glee at this "candy book" gift—even though he'd gotten the same thing for several years in a row.

I wish I could say I remember his name, but I don't. I wish I could say I'd thought of him off and on since graduating from elementary school, but I hadn't—until I ran across another "candy book" just a few days ago.

What I do remember is that I had serious suspicions that Mr. Bus Driver was really Santa Claus and that driving the school bus was just something he did between Christmases, because to my 9-year-old eyes, he looked very old. (Which probably means he was all of 35.)

And I remember that he let me sit on the seat right behind his so I could read. I loved to read, you see, but I also was prone to motion sickness—especially if seated at the back of a big, swaying school bus. When I told him this during the first week of his being my bus driver, he could have reacted with horror and told me to stop reading on the bus. Instead, he calmly designated the seat right behind him as my seat, so I could read queasiness-free—even though, back then, school bus seating wasn't assigned.

And I remember that he was always eating hard candy.

So, when it was time to get teacher gifts, and I discovered a "candy book" with a Santa on the cover, I decided that teacher gifts included bus-driver gifts, and gave this perfect gift to my Santa-Claus-look-alike, hard-candy-eating, reader-promoting bus driver.

Which may well be the only "perfect" gift I've ever given. On the other hand, my elementary school bus driver is still giving a gift to me.

Because a few days ago, after all those memories came back, I bought that "candy book" for myself. And while I'm scurrying around on just one more Christmas shopping errand—which, I admit, I won't be able to resist—I'll just have a hard candy and think of Mr. Bus Driver and try to remember what he knew year-round: the best gifts can't be bought.

(December 23, 2002)

~♥~

Daughter takes the cake, so I'll have the icing

My 10-turning-11-year-old's pronouncement is shocking: she doesn't want icing on her birthday cake.

To me, a cake is just an excuse to hold up the icing... the more icing the better. In fact, for my own birthday each year I wonder if I ought to save my husband and kids the trouble of baking my cake and tell them just to pop open a can of ready-made icing and stick a candle straight in. Just dig in with spoons, and off we go.

So for me, it is impossible to imagine someone wanting a cake without icing. Especially someone I very clearly recall giving birth to.

When I ask her why she doesn't want icing on her birthday cake, her explanation is simple—she doesn't like icing any more.

Somehow, I find her straightforward explanation hard to accept. I've always iced her birthday cakes. So I start looking for alternate explanations.

What if as a pre-teen she's already worrying too much about her looks, even though she's a healthy weight? But no, there she is, helping herself to seconds at dinner.

What if her cake preference is due to peer pressure over some sort of weird anti-icing fad? But no, there she is, with other kids at another party who happily accept her offering of scraped off icing from her cake.

It seems that she truly doesn't like icing—and that I'm going to have to bake her an icing-less birthday cake.

I decide, though, to try a different recipe. Somehow making our usual family birthday cake recipe without icing seems like a betrayal of all those happy, icing-filled memories of birthdays past. I settle on a chocolate bundt cake, because the recipe has the word "Easy" in its title and because bundt cakes usually aren't iced.

Now, I've made all kinds of cakes before without a problem—even ones with "Difficult" in their titles. Even other bundt cakes. But not only does the first bundt cake collapse with a wooshing sound as I pull it from the oven, the second one does too.

I'm not sure what went wrong. Maybe I was distracted by memories of my daughter on her first birthday, gleefully smooshing her birthday cupcake—and all its glorious icing—into her face. In any case, by the time the second bundt cake collapses, I realize I don't have enough time to run to the grocery for more bundt cake ingredients before the birthday girl gets home from school. But I do have just enough time and ingredients to make one regular, icing-less chocolate cake—which is what she wanted in the first place.

Later, as I glance at my daughter happily eating a piece of icing-less birthday cake, I realize what the collapsing bundt cakes were trying to tell me as they sighed "woosh."

I'm not really bothered by icing or the lack thereof. I'm just coping with the fact that my daughter's hit the right age for asserting opinions I just don't get. And such differences of opinion surely won't remain over topics as trivial as icing.

There's only one solution. Accept it. And get myself my own personal cans of icing on her future birthdays. (January 13, 2003)

~♥~

Dancing on Mardi Gras

Tomorrow is Mardi Gras—the day for a last fling of festivity before the Lenten season.

Tomorrow I'll smile at the news reports of feisty Mardi Gras revelers down in New Orleans. But I'll also relish a Mardi Gras memory that every year gives me a dash of insight into the meaning of the holiday at the other end of Lent.

Flashback: I'm 22; a newlywed in New Orleans. My husband and I attend an uptown Methodist church with a tiny congregation and no organist. I volunteer to play a few simple songs on the church's lovely, old pipe organ each week. I'm not an organist, but I've been trained on the piano, and the organ would otherwise sit silent.

Most Sundays, a quiet middle-aged man named John slips into a back pew by himself. But one mid-February Sunday, he comes with his 15-year-old daughter, who is enchanted by the organ. After service, John wonders if I'll show his daughter the organ. Sure, I say.

The following Sunday, John tells me he has a little thank you gift... an invitation for my husband and me to a Mardi Gras ball. John, it turns out, is king of one of the Mardi Gras Krewes that put on parades and host private balls.

I'm overwhelmed. All I did was spend a half-hour showing his daughter the pipe organ. And being invited to a Mardi Gras ball is a big deal, a matter of having the right social connections—which we don't. We're just young Yankee newlyweds, still in college.

At 22, I'm still naive enough to believe that people fall into two categories: most of us, and a much smaller group of "them—" people who are always happy and problem-free. The kind of people who are Kings of Mardi Gras krewes. The kind of people who get invited to Mardi Gras balls. Hey... that's us!

The ball is held in a beautifully decorated party hall. There's a jazz band. Good food. Much revelry.

I start talking with someone who knows Krewe-King John well. She tells me that John owns a large company—he is, in fact, a millionaire. And every year, he makes sure that at least half of his Mardi Gras ball guests are people who would otherwise never get invited. People of modest means, or suffering health problems, or in some other way—to use her word—broken.

That's when it hits me. My husband and I are in the broken half of the crowd.

Bitterness threatens to overtake my joy. After all, I don't want to be one of the broken people. I want to be one of the mythical "them—" the always happy, the problem-free.

Then I hear the rest of the story. John invites "broken" people, the woman says, as a way of showing thanks for all he's achieved—although he hasn't always had it easy. For example, he's just gone through a divorce—and almost lost his relationship with his daughter in the process. But, for some reason, things are better now. Something about his daughter being so excited over trying out a church organ on a recent weekend visit, that she forgot her bitterness and had a great time with her dad.

Before I can really take in what the woman has told me, John organizes all of us in a big circle to do a conga dance. The fourth or fifth dizzying time around, I glimpse our King-of-the-Krewe smiling, his laughing daughter dancing right behind him.

And in a flash, I realize something that I remember every Mardi Gras:

All of us are broken.

Yet, with a little grace from one another, all of us can dance.

(March 3, 2003)

~♥~

Their "winning" season

The pizza is ordered. The soda pop has been poured. The girls are busily signing and decorating the backs of each other's team T-shirts, turning the whole process into a giggle-fest.

During this end-of-the-basketball-season get-together, all I have to do is chat with the other parents while waiting for my mushroom pizza.

But I'm having trouble focusing. It's not the giggles themselves that distract me. It's my wonderment that these girls, at this particular end-of-season party, are able to giggle at all, to cut up with each other, to act like the buddies they've become.

They are, after all, showing the high spirits of winners.

But... they're losers. At least, in basketball; at least, according to their team's dead-last finish in their league. And they didn't lose by just a little. Their team lost each of its first few games by 20 points: a lot for any game; an enormous margin in fifth-/sixth grade basketball where the top score might be 20 points.

Part of the scoring deficit came from inexperience—this team had the greatest percentage of first-time players in the league. And after those first few games—when three of the girls quit—part of it was having a smaller roster than the other teams.

So, by our culture's winning-is-all standards—these girls should *not* be giggling. They should be weeping in their root beers.

After all, losers are not supposed to be joyous. Oh, it's OK to lose for a little while; who doesn't, after all, love the story of a losing team that comes back to win it all at a tournament in the last few seconds? But mostly, we try to bury our losses deep down in memory, while we proudly display our winning trophies.

So what happened? I doubt any of the girls read *My Losing Season*, the memoir in which novelist Pat Conroy recreates his collegiate senior year's losing season and the effect it had on him and on many of his classmates, even decades later.

And I doubt I really influenced my daughter to take a philosophical view of her team's situation. Sure, I told her a few times at the beginning of the season that often you learn more from losing than from winning. She took my comments with all the grace of a pre-teen: marathon eye-rolling; long, grumpy silences. No one likes to lose, for pity's sake.

Yet, in his memoir, Conroy reminds us that compared to winning, "Loss is a fiercer, more uncompromising teacher, coldhearted but clear-eyed in its understanding that life is more dilemma than game, and more trial than free pass."

Somehow, the seven girls who stuck to the team figured this out by themselves. By the end of the season, they were playing as a real team. No ball hogs. No eye-rolling or long, grumpy silences (on court, anyway). No whining at refs or coaches. When a play went well, the whole team cheered. When someone messed up, the whole team told her—it's OK; you'll get it next time.

So while the girls giggled and I waited for pizza, I thought about how different this season was than last season for my daughter. Last season, my daughter was on the league's winning team. And her coach told her, "This is the team you'll never forget!"

I hope he's wrong.

I hope that this year's losing team is the one she—and her teammates—will always remember.

(March 17, 2003)

~♥~

Thinking 'om,' but getting z's

I recently read that because of these "tense times" (have there ever been "relaxed times?") more and more Americans are giving meditation a try. Let's be honest: this is a fad that'll disappear faster than a post-90's mutual fund. If we can't master the technique in 10-steps-or-less from a book-on-tape during rush hour, forget it.

On the other hand, meditation does sound so soothing... finally finding that "om" of true inner peace...

plus I never like to let a good fad pass me by. So I decide to give meditation a try.

Or rather, another try. See, I took a meditation class some 20 years ago. And flunked. Because three minutes into the first session, I dozed off. Snoring in the middle of a meditation class does not, I assure you, win points with the instructor.

Still, I decide to try to remember all the stuff I learned in those three minutes and meditate one night. I take a shower, don my comfiest jammies, sit cross-legged on my bed, hold my hands palm-up, and focus on my breathing, which is supposed to clear my mind so I can think about absolutely... nothing.

The first thing I think is... dang, I breath loudly.

So I repeat the little mantra I learned 20 years ago for "re-centering" whenever thoughts stray from nothing to something: Relaxation in... (inhale); tension out... (exhale).

The next thing I think is where is this perky little tone of voice coming from? I never think in perky little tones. I think in frantic streams, as in, oh-no-the-bologna's-spoiled-now-what-to-do-for-lunch-tomorrow-and-is-that-a-cat-I-hear-locked-in-the-closet...

My perky little voice becomes a mite peevish: Relaxation in! Tension out!

Uh oh. It is the voice of... my former meditation instructor. This, frankly, unnerves me.

In fact, I'm so totally distracted I think, fine, I might as well take a break and set my hair in curlers. Sort of super-size my meditation with a side of beauty treatments.

I'm a breath-and-a-half into meditating in my curlers, when I hear a loud pounding at my bedroom door and, "What are you doing in there?"

This is not the voice of my former instructor. This is the voice of my daughter.

"Meditating!" I snap. "Finding the 'om' of my inner peace..."

"But mommmmm, you said we could do a manicure tonight!"

Fine. If I'm going to have my hands flopping in the air anyway, I might as well do my nails and let them air dry. A little meditative multi-tasking never hurt anyone, right?

A half hour later, my daughter and I each have Mocha Mauve Medley-tipped nails. My daughter leaves to go view the latest Lizzie McGuire TV show. I go back to meditating.

My breathing still seems loud, while the visiting inner voice of my meditation instructor now has passed from peevish to perturbed—"Relaxation! IN! Tension! OUT!"

But then, suddenly, the voice is replaced by a long, low, warm sound... finally, the 'om' of true inner peace! No... wait... that's the cat, who's escaped from the closet and is now purring while rubbing against my freshly painted nails.

"Ignore that!" screams that inner voice. "RELAXATION IN!"

I tell the voice to shut up. I toss the cat off the bed. And then I decide I knew what I was doing all along, 20 years ago.

I'm taking a nap—furry fingernails and all.
(April 14, 2003)

~♥~

A wagon full of treasure

Junk pick-up day was last week in my neighborhood—the day the city kindly picks up all the trash it would normally leave curbside on regular trash pick-up days: pooped refrigerators, de-flamed grills. And so on.

I try to follow the "three Rs" of environmental conscientiousness—reduce, reuse, recycle—but it seems there's always something each year that's truly outlived its usefulness and must simply be thrown away.

So we hauled to our curb a chair whose spring had sprung and a broken-down, 10-year-old printer. My husband went inside; I went in the garage and started eyeing my kids' little red plastic wagon.

My kids are 9 and 11 and haven't used the wagon for two years. It has a crack in the side, and its wheels wobble, so it's not fit as a hand-me-down or donation. And for the past few years, its only function has been as an unwieldy shelf-on-wheels for soccer balls and basketballs. Plus, it seems to always be annoyingly in the way of the lawn mower.

Now would be a good time to get rid of it, I thought, and finally have easy access to the lawn mower—but still, I hesitated. I'm a sentimental sap when it comes to getting rid of my kids' stuff. So instead of just dragging the wagon to the curb, I stared at it, remembering my little girls taking turns pulling each other along the sidewalk, before bikes and rollerblades and scooters charmed them away from the simple pleasure of a wagon.

As I hesitated, two things happened at once. Someone in a truck pulled up curbside to peer at my neighbors junk across the street—a more appealing pile than mine, featuring some decent looking shelves, for example.

And my kids rollerbladed/scooted into my driveway. "What're those folks doing across the street?" asked the 9-year-old.

"They're pickers," I explained. "Folks on junk days like to go around, take a look at what's curbside."

"Why do they do that?" asked the 11-year-old.

I shrugged. "See if they can reuse it or maybe sell it for scrap. Ever hear the old saying, one person's trash is another person's treasure?"

In fact, last year, I'd plucked a big wicker basket from a neighbor's pile. I cleaned it up, refreshed it with a coat of spray paint, and now use it as the perfect-sized laundry basket for kitchen towels. But before I could launch into this example of junk-day-picking cleverness, my kids were dumping out the balls from their forgotten wagon.

"What are you doing?" I asked.

"We're going junk-picking!" said one.

"Yeah—looking for treasure!" said the other.

A half hour or so later, I saw them coming up the sidewalk—the 11-year-old pulling the wagon, in which little sis was riding and guarding their newfound treasures from the neighborhood trash piles. They excitedly showed me the contents of their little red wagon: an unopened pack of 500 sheets of notebook paper (for summer art projects and note writing!) and about 30 pinecones (just add peanut butter and birdseed for birdfeeders!) and the best prize of all: a huge roll of bubble wrap! Ah, the joy of popping bubbles on bubble wrap...

They put their treasures away and went inside for baths. I looked at the wagon. I looked at the other junk by my curb.

And I put the wagon right where it still belongs for now.

By the lawn mower.

(June 16, 2003)

~♥~

Houseplant anarchy

My houseplants have fleas. And it's all Spike's fault.

I love houseplants. The problem is, in my house, prayer plants just don't have a prayer. Jade plants quickly become jaded. Spider plants crawl off to die. Palm plants have very short lifelines. And bonsai go samurai.

That is actually Rocky's fault. I know it's not because I have a black thumb, because Rocky is very healthy. Rocky is also the first houseplant I ever owned, a pothos ivy I got in college, 20-some years ago. I named it after the Rocky of movie fame, wanting my plant to survive no matter what punches life threw at it. And thrive Rocky has, with healthy green tendrils that stretch four feet long.

The problem is, since then, every plant I've brought home has kicked the bucket—er, ceramic pot.

Surely it's not my black thumb—look at how healthy Rocky is. I suspect Rocky. Does he hop over in the middle of the night to give a one-two punch to the other plants? Did I expose little Rocky too soon to *Little Shop of Horrors* (one of my favorite movies, in which a plant from outer space turns murderous)?

Then along came Harry, a baby 6-inch weeping fig. I brought it home, feeling just a wee bit guilty that I was condemning it to certain death—but surprise! It survived! For 15 whole years! And now it's 6-feet tall!

The only explanation I can come up with is that Rocky got lonely and decided Harry made a good friend. And for several years, since Harry and Rocky got along so well, I decided to leave well enough alone.

But a few months ago, I saw Spike at a flea market, and my heart melted. The little snake plant looked so cute with its two blades poking up out of its pot. And, the guy at the flea market assured me <u>nothing</u> can kill a snake plant. Not even Rocky, I thought? Hmmm... Spike would be a good name for this little snake plant... You know how it is. Once you've named a plant, it's yours.

So I paid a buck, put little two-bladed Spike carefully in my passenger seat, and started the drive home.

By the time I got there, one of Spike's blades had completely flopped over. And by the time I got Spike in the house, the blade had fallen off. And the poor thing hadn't even met Rocky yet.

But Spike had brought along his own little army. Fleas. From the flea market, you see. The fleas didn't bother Spike, who quickly grew a bunch of healthy new blades. Rocky and Harry, however, started looking a little, well, droopy.

It was time for professional help. These three were going to have to call a truce. I went to a garden shop and told the nice lady that my houseplants have fleas, and it's Spike's fault, and the fleas are making Harry and Rocky sick, which I really don't appreciate, even though Rocky has used his long tendrils to choke to death all kinds of other houseplants in the middle of the night because I exposed poor Rocky to *Little Shop of Horrors* at too young of an age...

The lady at the garden shop stared at me (as if I'm nuts, for some reason), then explained that no, my houseplants do not have fleas. They have fungus gnats and I just need to spray them with houseplant insecticide. Knowing how to take care of plants, she assured me, is a matter of acquiring scientific knowledge... not naming them and assigning them personality traits.

Well, maybe. Still, while spraying them, I told Spike, Harry and Rocky that they'd better behave and get along because you never know. In 15 years, I might actually get another houseplant.

(June 23, 2003)

~♥~

How do you trash a trash can?

How do you throw away a trash can?

This is not a rhetorical question. This is a serious inquiry, based on 4 weeks of attempting to throw away 3 large trash cans.

Of course, throwing away a tiny trash can is simple. You just stuff it into a larger trash can. The problem is, the last time I threw away a tiny trash can, the entire house got redecorated.

See, my spiffy new trash can was somewhere between a bisque and a taupe, which clashed with the background color to the border in my home office. So, the border needed replaced, but first the walls needed repainted to match the hues of the border, and once all of that was done, I realized the hall wall color disconcertingly clashed with my office wall color, so that needed repainting, and of course the hall leads to other rooms plus the stairs that lead downstairs, and the new wall color clashed with the trim color, and the trim is right by the carpet, which was off just a shade...

Perhaps I shouldn't have been surprised that when I suggested we might want to replace our three 10-year-old household trashcans, my husband went pale and gasped, "Are you s-s-sure? Think of their sentimental value."

"They're so old, they leak. We leave a little trail behind us whenever we drag them to the curb," I said. "Besides, am I really supposed to belief you're sentimental about a trio of trashcans?"

"You're right," he admitted. "I just don't want to have to repaint the whole house..."

When we were reduced to asking the neighbors if they might rent us some space in *their* trash cans, he finally agreed we should replace the trashcans.

Which brings us back to our non-rhetorical question: how do you throw away a trash can?

The first week, we tried making signs, taped to the trashcan lids: Please throw away trash AND cans! Thank you!

It rained. The signs dissolved. The trash cans stayed.

The second week, we had new signs laminated and super-glued them to the trash can lids.

A windstorm ensued. The lids blew away. The trash cans stayed.

The third week, we took turns waiting up all night for the trash collectors... but we dozed off. We ran down the street hollering, "Please! Take our trash cans AND our trash!"

But we were too late. The trash cans stayed. We decided we were stuck with the trash cans.

However, luck was with us. The trash collectors came later than usual the fourth week, happening by as I was putting something out in the mailbox.

The nice trash collector looked at my oozing, moaning, pathetic trash cans, then looked at me and said, "ma'am, we—the city's entire maintenance department, that is— have been wondering... are these cans containers for your trash, or part of your trash?"

I bet that's the first time that nice trash collector's been hugged by a woman (weeping with joy) who's unrelated to him while she's still in her bathrobe and sipping coffee.

So, finally, by this stroke of luck, our trash cans were gone. My husband bought replacements, and beamed as only a man can about such a purchase.

"Aren't these beauts? Power-pro snap-lock lids. Titanium-based, 40 p.s.i. wheels..."

At least, he was beaming until I said, "Just wondering...
do you think the new trash cans clash with the garage door
color?"

(June 30, 2003)

~♥~

Clean life makes Mom dog-tired

A few days after we got our new dog, I laid down the
law: a never-before-experienced, super-sanitized cleanliness
shall reign upon our household!

This was because I discovered that when a beagle
shakes himself, fur flies everywhere. Including onto the
table and countertop.

So, I called everyone together and proclaimed: We
shall clean and sanitize the kitchen countertop and table
with disinfectant before cooking/dining!

We shall have color coded sponges—the pink one for
cleaning the cat/dog food bowls, the blue one for cleaning
countertop/table... and of course the sponges shall be
sanitized in hot water after each use!

And we shall teach the dog the all-important
commands—Down! and Sit!—so that said dog shall refrain
from begging in the kitchen or at the table!

After I proclaimed these quite reasonable
commandments, several things happened.

The kids and husband gave each other long, knowing
looks.

The cats snickered.

The dog hid.

Still, I persevered.

And made it through an entire day, following my own rules. Then, as I stood in my kitchen, proudly surveying its sparkling clean, super-sanitized floor and countertop and sink, my 11-year-old daughter came in and said, "Mom, weren't we supposed to make deviled eggs for the church potluck tomorrow?"

As we boiled eggs, the dog came into the kitchen. I said, "Sit!" He did, on my super-sanitized floor. Then gave me a look that barked, "Lady, I'm not so sure about living here, you know?"

My daughter and I cut the boiled eggs in half (on our super-sanitized cutting block), and put the yolks in a small (super-sanitized) measuring cup.

My daughter started mashing (with a super-sanitized fork) mayo and mustard and seasonings into the egg yolks. The dog, licking his lips, stood on his hind legs. "Down!" I said. So, he lay down and heaved a weary, bedeviled sigh.

And for the first time that day, I could empathize with the dog. After all my cleaning and sanitizing, I was weary, too.

So I said to my daughter, with years-of-cooking wisdom, "Dearie, let your smart, ol' mama show you a little short-cut!"

I got out the mixer and put just one beater in the small measuring cup that held the egg yolk/mayo/mustard.

The dog stood again.

And I took my hand from the measuring cup handle to point at him and say, "Sit!" just as I turned on the mixer thus turning the little measuring cup into a madly spinning Tasmanian devil that wildly flung egg yolk everywhere—on the floor, the counter, the ceiling, my daughter, me, the dog... Desperately, I yelled at the mixer: "Down! Sit!"

It didn't heed my plea, and neither did the dog, who happily jumped up and down in a little dog dance, while yipping a little dog song: Yip, yip, hurray! At last, cleanliness is not reigning! But deviled eggs are—raining, that is! Doggy manna from heaven!

My daughter unplugged the mixer.

I picked up the blue super-sanitized sponge.

And the dog eyed me with a look that woofed, "hey, maybe you're OK after all!" then started licking up deviled egg yolks from the floor. I'm so glad I sanitized it for him. (September 8, 2003)

~♥~

Windows from past become a real present
My history lesson—though somewhat sketchy in the details—was all prepared for our trip downtown.

And I started giving it to my kids before we even entered the Schuster Performing Arts Center, as we stepped out of the parking garage and crossed the street.

I pointed to the building and said, "Before the Schuster stood here, there was a large department store called Lazarus..."

My 10-year-old looked confused. "That's in the mall."

"Yeah," said the 11-year-old. "Everyone knows there are no department stores downtown."

"Well, once-upon-a-time there were," I said, as we stepped up on the sidewalk. "And on this very spot was Lazarus, which before that was Shilito-Rike's, which before *that* was just Rike's..."

But my kids were staring up at the building, saying something to each other. I gave them the mama's-telling-you-something-important-now-pay-attention glare. They snapped to attention.

"We were just saying this is a really cool looking building," said the 11-year-old.

"Yeah," said the 10-year-old as we entered the building. "So what did the Rike's building look like?"

"Tall. And rectangular." My kids did not look impressed. "And it was blown up to clear the space for this building," I added.

Things blowing up usually impresses kids this age. But their exclamations of "cool!" were not in response to my history lesson. Their "cools" were in reaction to the soaring

Schuster ceilings, the impressive windows, the spiraling staircase and balcony.

Several "cools" later, I said "ahem." My kids snapped to again.

"As I was saying," I continued, "the old Rike's store had exterior windows, usually filled with displays of items for sale, but at Christmas, the windows were filled with wonderful Christmas scenes. It was called the Holiday Toy Shop display and was started in the 1950s..."

"That's, like, 50 years ago," my 11-year-old said. "I thought you said this would be cool!" She and her sister exchanged glances—and I knew what they were thinking. Anything that was cool 50 years ago couldn't possibly be cool now.

And for a moment, my heart dropped. The old Rike's display I only vaguely remembered had moving figures and impressive attention to detail and colorful backdrops—still great stuff when I was a kid 30 years ago. But my kids are children of the special-effects age. How could these kids possibly be thrilled by moving mannequins of toy-making-elves and night-before-Christmas children?

I sighed. "Come on," I said, now just wanting to get this over with. We walked over to a large wood framed case that held one of the window scenes, a cozy Victorian-era family.

"Kids, try to understand that these scenes are a special part of Dayton history. The scenes were on display until the

1980s and it's really nice that the Schuster has brought them back..."

But my kids still weren't interested in my history lesson. They were peering in the window, charmed by the cozy scene.

No "cools" were exclaimed. Just simple, heartfelt sighs of pleasure. And young, strong hands eagerly tugging me to the next window.

History lesson forgotten, I watched my kids take in scenes from holidays past and thought... what a lovely present.

(December 22, 2003)

~♥~

SHARON SHORT

84

CHAPTER 4

~❤~

The Dog Ate My Lipstick

Meet Stuart... and Butterscotch

Four words I swore I'd never use as an empowered mom: "Go ask your father."

And yet, when my 12-year-old asked me: "Can we go to the pet store for a mouse? It's for a science fair project my friend and I are doing. We want to teach a mouse to go through a color-coded maze to find cheese..." somehow, those four fateful little words slipped from my lips.

Maybe I was just too tired to deal with my 12-year-old's inevitable disappointment at my "no." Besides, my husband swears that our house is already a suburban version of *Wild Kingdom*, what with the beagle, three cats, and one very nervous fish. Plus we've both nixed the 10-year-old's repeated pleas for a guinea pig.

So I knew he'd say "no way" to the mouse... and then I could be the hero and merrily suggest another experiment that didn't involve a long-term commitment to a rodent. Say, something to do with seeds in a paper cup.

He said, "Yes."

Not only that, but he proclaimed the science fair experiment "a great idea."

Maybe he was just distracted, because for some reason, he then took off for the office to catch up on paperwork— and he didn't seem to hear me shrieking from the back door.

Anyway, that's how I found myself taking the 12-year-old and her co-conspirator (who already has two horses, two dogs, a hamster and a goat... so a mouse at *her* house, my daughter explained, would create some serious crowding issues) to the pet store.

In the pet store parking lot, I lectured the two 12-year-olds... "Now, you understand, we're only renting the mouse, so to speak. Just for the duration of the science fair experiment. Then we're returning the mouse."

"Oh, sure, we understand," the two 12-year-old mad scientists solemnly promised.

I'd already double-checked and the helpful pet store employee swore I could return the mouse—if it was still healthy—although I wouldn't get back my $1.99 plus tax.

Which was fine with me. I would have paid the store $20 to take back the mouse.

We went into the pet store. "Ooh, the mice are soooooo cute," squealed my daughter and her friend.

My heart slipped a notch.

"Lots of people must keep mice for pets," said my daughter. "Look at all the mice for sale."

"Actually," said the helpful pet store employee, "snake owners like to buy them, too. As food."

My heart plummeted faster than an elevator with mice-gnawed cables.

My daughter looked at me with big, brown, moist eyes and said, "If I could keep this little mouse, I'd name him Stuart. As in Stuart Little. As in the book you read us when we were little..."

Which is how I went from "go ask your dad," to "rent-a-mouse for science," to a literary pet mouse—and shelling out 40 bucks for mouse food and housing and exercise toys—in 58 minutes and 23 seconds flat. I think that's some kind of record—for being suckered.

A few hours later, my husband came home from work. And the 10-year-old asked him why big sis could get a mouse when we'd always said no to her pleas for a guinea pig.

Maybe he was just too tired to deal with the 10-year-old's disappointment at yet another "no." Because for the first time, he uttered four words he swore he'd never use as an empowered dad: "Go ask your mom."

The guinea pig's name is Butterscotch.

(February 23, 2004)

~♥~

Jumping through hoops with the family dog

Six months after getting our dog, we decided he needed to go to doggie school.

Up to that point, Cosmo only responded well to two commands: "Jump!" and "Eat!" —not exactly things you have to teach a beagle.

At our first class—before the instructor even entered the cement-floored room—all the other dogs were already practicing rolling over and sitting. A shepherd and a Labrador were conferring on their paw pilots about play dates. Show offs, I thought, as Cosmo trotted over to the wall, decorated with a lovely mural of a park filled with dogs and bushes and trees, and lifted his leg to anoint a particularly nicely-rendered bush.

"Don't worry," said the shepherd's owner. "You have a beagle. No one expects too much."

As I finished cleaning up Cosmo's mess, the instructor came in and told us that for our dogs to graduate, they'd have to learn to respond to commands like "here" and "sit" and "stay."

"What about 'jump'?" I asked.

"Quiet!" Well, *she* sure had the command thing down.

She added that our dogs would, furthermore, have to learn a trick—such as "shake" or "roll over."

"What about 'jump'?" I insisted. Someone must have taught me the "persist" command early in life.

"Only through hoops," the instructor said.

Ye-e-es! If there was a treat awaiting him on the other side of the hoop, I knew Cosmo would go through it, even if it were on fire. Yeah! A flaming hoop! Cosmo could wear a cape, jump through flaming hoops, transform into Beagle Knievel! That'd show everyone.

Back home, I got out my kids' Hula-Hoop. "Here, Cosmo!" He whimpered and ran the other way, tail between legs.

Apparently, at some point in the year and a half before he became ours, Cosmo was traumatized by a mad attack Hula-Hoop. No way would he jump through hoops for me, not even to redeem us at doggie school.

Still, I refused to give up—that "persist" command again—although I doused the flaming hoop idea. First, I left the Hula-Hoop in the middle of the kitchen floor for a few days. To get to his food bowl, Cosmo had to walk around the hoop.

Once he was OK with that, I started leaving treats in the middle of the Hula-Hoop. Eventually, his stomach overcame his fears.

Next came holding up the Hula-Hoop and coaxing Cosmo to simply walk through it. And after that was OK with Cosmo, I finally tried holding the Hula-Hoop off the floor and hollering, "Jump!"

Fast forward to graduation night. Cosmo barely made it through "Sit" and "Stay," while the other dogs gave stellar performances. Show offs.

But then it was trick time. The other dogs shook. Rolled over. Played dead. (Yawn.)

Finally, it was Cosmo's turn. I held up the Hula-Hoop in one hand, knee high. I held a treat in my other hand. Cosmo sat on the non-treat side. I commanded, "Jump!" and he gave a joyous jump through the hoop, then sat down and looked at me expectantly. I gave him the treat. He gobbled it up, even without me commanding, "eat!"

Ta da! Cosmo's trick meant he graduated from doggie school!

Which makes me darned proud of my dog (and me), even as I wonder, which one of us was really jumping through hoops?

(March 8, 2004)

~♥~

Tooth be told, growing up can be painful
We're all familiar with the saying, "like pulling teeth," as in, "difficult to do."

The phrase seems custom-made for pre-teens, as in, "Getting Jr. to clean his room was like pulling teeth."

Or, in our family's case, "Getting the 12-year-old to pull her tooth was like... pulling teeth."

Now, to be fair, I have no right to whine, dentally speaking. My kids have no cavities. They floss without complaint. They only demand a buck-a-tooth from the tooth fairy.

What more could I want?

For my 12-year-old's last baby tooth to fall out, that's what.

Our dentist put braces on my 12-year-old's teeth, even with one extremely wiggly baby tooth in place, and gave me a complex orthodontic lecture about why this made sense. I just folded my arms and predicted that he'd end up having to pull the baby tooth. Somehow, a mama just knows.

And sure enough, my 12-year-old, who had been gleeful about every lost tooth in the past, became suddenly indifferent to wiggling this one.

"Wiggle," I pled, threatened, bribed, cajoled, and moaned.

"It'll come out when it wants to," said she of the orange-wired-brackets.

"Wiggle it out, dear, or I'll have to pull it next visit," the dentist said to my daughter a week or so ago.

She just shrugged again, and picked out pink wires.

"Told ya so, told ya so," I taunted the dentist. OK, not really. But my daughter's reaction didn't really surprise me. Losing that final baby tooth—how bittersweet! A pre-teen wouldn't say that. Somehow, a mama just knows.

Still, it needed to go. And I didn't want the dentist to have to pull it. I was desperate to find a way to convince my 12-year-old to wiggle that last tooth.

A few days later, my 10-year-old unwittingly paved the way with her proclamation: "I have FOUR wiggly teeth!"

"Aww... Your last four baby teeth," I sighed.

"You're not sentimental about MY last baby tooth," my 12-year-old said.

"Go wiggle right now, missy!"

That was directed to my 12-year-old, but my 10-year-old listened. The next morning, even before breakfast, she lost a tooth.

"Show off," said my 12-year-old.

"Wiggle!" I said.

The 12-year-old rolled her eyes, but my 10-year-old heeded my order. By noon she'd pulled a second tooth.

"Whatever," said my 12-year-old.

"Wiggle!" I said.

So... (I'm not kidding...) by dinnertime, my 10-year-old pulled a *third* tooth.

At which point, I looked at my 12-year-old and did something I swore I'd never do. I invoked sibling rivalry.

"You know," I said, "this means you and your little sister are now tied for who will first lose all her baby teeth."

An hour later, I was presented with yet another just-pulled tooth. This one, though, was from my 12-year-old, who was beaming. "Hah! I won!" she said.

That night, the tooth fairy and I lost four bucks and shed a few tears.

And the next morning, when my 10-year-old said thoughtfully, "You know, that fourth tooth isn't as wiggly as I thought. I think I'll keep it for awhile," I just smiled and nodded and said, "Good idea."

Getting me to change my mind would be like, well, pulling teeth.

(April 5, 2004)

~♥~

Revenge of the beagle

Timing is everything, or so the saying goes.

Unfortunately for our beagle, Cosmo, our timing in adopting him coincided perfectly with our daughters' timing in deciding they were too "old" to still dress up and make up their dolls.

This new pre-teen rule doesn't apply, however, to the family dog. Their first effort in dressing the dog is fairly innocuous: a doggie sweater. Navy blue. Gold appliqué anchor on the lapel. This ensemble makes him look perky. Which is a rather extraordinary feat, for a hound.

My husband is not impressed. If the dog could speak, he says, Cosmo's opinion would be 'leave me au naturelle.'

The mature adult in me agrees… but then I flash on a memory of when I was about eleven and, like my daughters, decided I was too "old" to dress up my dolls. My new pre-teen rule didn't apply, however, to the family cat. So I put him in a bonnet and rode around the neighborhood with him in my bike basket.

I share this precious memory with my husband. He moans. Don't worry, I say. The cat scratch scars have long faded.

I'm not worried about that, he says. It's just that I foresee our daughters following in your footsteps. First, dressing dolls. Then pets. Next they'll obsess about their own clothes, then someday try to tell their husbands how to dress.

Don't be silly, I say. And suggest his gray sweater would go better with his black pants than the navy one. But in solidarity with Cosmo, he keeps on the navy sweater.

Several months pass. Cosmo wears his sweater without scratching, whining or snapping. Spring comes along, and my daughters and I go to the salon for hair appointments. And on the salon's reception desk, we see the cutest display of Pawlish. Nail polish for pets… tested on people, not animals, proclaim the bottles.

Ohhh… please? my daughters plea.

The mature adult in me knows I should say "no." But somehow, the 11-year-old-who-dressed-her-unneutered-male-cat-in-bonnets springs forth and says... OK. We settle on "Doghouse Blue Pawlish" which will, we think, coordinate well with the navy sweater.

Husband is even less impressed. If the dog could speak, he says, Cosmo's opinion would be "keep your mitts off my paws." But Cosmo accepts his manicure... or would that be dogicure?... without scratching, whining or snapping.

A few weeks later, we're all reading various parts of the newspaper (kids, comics; hubby, Sports; me, Life section), when I come across an article about using Kool-Aid to naturally (but not permanently) dye a pet's fur during a routine bath.

I share this idea. It's non-toxic, I say. Could be fun. Yeah, our daughters say; let's tint Cosmo's white patches blue! To match his sweater! And his dogicure pawlish!

Husband is now appalled. If that poor dog could speak, he says, Cosmo's opinion would be... Crunch, crunch, crunch. The sound's coming from upstairs. We look around, realize Cosmo has quietly left the living room.

We rush upstairs... and there they are. Two tubes of lip-gloss and one of lipstick, thoroughly chewed up and spat out, right in front of the bathroom door. Cosmo sitting right by the plundered tubes. Glaring up at us.

My daughters and I are appalled. Those were our favorite shades!

But my husband is grinning. I think, he says, that Cosmo finally gave his opinion... so to speak.

Coincidence? Perhaps. Or proof that timing really is everything.

(April 26, 2004)

~♥~

The scariest ride of all

I have discovered the scariest amusement park ride of all time.

No amusement park ride engineer—or whatever you call people who create rides and roller coasters—could possibly come up with anything scarier.

This is the Jason, the *Friday the 13th*, the *Nightmare on Elm Street* amusement park ride. A ride that would scare Stephen King into penning romantic haikus for the rest of his career. And if you happen to live near me, this ride is closer than you think—just down the road at Paramount's Kings Island.

Don't think you're safe if you happen to be reading this from some other locale than the greater Dayton, Ohio area. This nightmare of a ride exists at most every amusement park in the world.

Perhaps you think I refer to The Beast, the longest wooden roller coaster in the world. Hah, I say. The ride I'm talking about seems to last an eternity.

Son of Beast, the "tallest, fastest and only looping wooden roller coaster on the planet?" Nah. The ride I'm talking about sent my head looping faster than anything any amusement park ride engineer could think up.

What about Drop Zone, which lifts riders up 26 stories high… then drops them all at once for 61 feet? Oh, puh-lease. A ride that makes your shoes fly off and shoves your heart up into your throat while turning your lungs inside out is nothing compared to the scary ride I discovered.

Then there are the rides that hold you upside down, or send you through corkscrew twists and loop-de-loops. Bah, I say.

All of these rides are mere child's play compared to the truly scariest ride ever. The first 20 seconds alone of this ride can create more gut wrenching, heart stopping, mind-bending fear than riding the tilt-a-whirl on double speed after consuming a Coney dog, cotton candy, and a super-sized cola.

I refer, of course, to the antique car track.

You say there's not a thing scary about riding around on a track in a car that's a souped-up riding lawn mower reconfigured to look like an old-fashioned automobile?

Well, that's what I thought, too… when I drove such a car when I was 12.

And later, when I rode on it with my single-digit-aged kids, I thought it was positively cute when they wanted to "steer." I even videotaped the event, still under the delusion that this was a non-scary ride.

Now I know better. This is because I went on this ride a weekend ago with my 12-year-old daughter.

It wasn't so bad that she insisted on driving.

Or that she tried to steer carefully to avoid jolting our souped-up-lawn-mower's wheels against the track.

What made the ride far more terrifying than anything that can flip, dip, drop, twist or twirl was that the whole time she drove, she kept talking about how she couldn't wait to get her driving learner's permit... in just three years, five months, and 13 days.

That it would be so cool to drive herself to her activities. Or drive her friends around. In our family car. It was the first time she'd ever talked about herself as a future driver. The kid's timing is incredible.

But it made me think: you know those padded body harnesses that straightjacket you in place so you can barely breathe, what's more move, on the wildest roller coasters?

I've already started my search for an amusement park ride engineer who can replace our car's seat belts with those.

(May 3, 2004)

~♥~

Very best gardens unplanned

This summer, as every summer before, I had a plan. And not just in my head. A real plan, complete with sketched designs and shopping lists.

Each front porch container would contain a spirea, three geraniums (fuchsia) and three petunias (white).

To the corner rose bed, I'd continue the geranium (fuchsia) and petunia (white) theme. Under the crab apple tree, at the end of the shrubs, I'd simply put mulch around the hostas. No impatiens, this year. Last year, the impatiens had gotten leggy and, frankly, I was getting... well... impatient with them.

I made similar plans for the containers on the deck (snap dragons) and our tiny vegetable garden (tomatoes, cucumbers, zucchini.)

Then, as so often happens... in fact, as it's happened every summer since I started doing a very modest bit of gardening... life interrupted my plans.

The first interruption came in the form of a lone marigold, given to me on Mother's Day by my 10-year-old, in a plastic cup decorated with hearts and swirls and smiley faces.

Note "marigolds" were not in my plan.

But, alas, my heart melted for this one marigold—what mother's heart wouldn't—and I thought surely one splash of yellow would not ruin my plans for an orderly, dignified fuchsia and white design?

The next interruption to my plans came in the form of a book deadline, which postponed my trip to the garden store. (But I kept nurturing that marigold on my kitchen windowsill.)

And the third interruption to my plans came from the 12-year-old who said, "We are going to have morning glories growing up the lamppost, right?"

I told her no, because the morning glories—which I planted five years ago as part of another "perfect" plan and which I've been trying to control every year since—have their own plan: taking over the front lawn. So this year, instead of pulling out all but a few, I was going to yank them all.

Finally, deadline met... lone marigold well-tended but lonely... I went to the garden store.

Where flats of marigolds flashed their sunny smiles at me. And zinnias suggested they'd happily reside with snapdragons in my deck containers, salvias beckoned with their dainty white and blue blossoms at me and made me forget about spirea, and impatiens pled for one more chance, promising to be bushy rather than leggy this season. Meanwhile, red petunias cried out for attention while the fuchsia petunias and the geraniums all said that, really, they'd rather go with a gardener who knows how to not only make plans, but also how to stick with them.

Since I'd gotten to the garden store so late in the season, the zucchini had all left with other gardeners, but an eggplant thought it could reside with the tomatoes and cucumbers, and a basil and bell pepper joined forces to point out that, really, once you've got eggplant and tomatoes, you might as well have basil and bell peppers so you can make eggplant Parmesan.

Then the morning glories chimed in, promising that if I planted them in containers, they wouldn't extend their tendrils to choke out all the other plants. Really.

My garden beds and containers are all planted now, bearing only the faintest resemblance to my original plans. They are far more riotous in color and variety... far more *unplanne*d... and, somehow, far more fun than my original plans.

Which makes me, and the now greatly befriended marigold, very happy.

(June 14, 2004)

~❤~

Jamming up a can-do spirit

Every summer, I engage in an arcane culinary art called: home canning.

Now, for those who know me, it's no doubt surprising that I voluntarily engage in home canning tomatoes, green beans, strawberries, peaches, cucumbers and so on. After all, I've been known to serve as dinner apple slices, cheese slices, popcorn and milk. So the kitchen is not exactly my usual domain of expertise.

But I grew up in a canning family. My grandmothers and great-grandmothers canned because that was the only way to ensure fruits and vegetables for their families during Appalachian winters. My mother canned to carry on a family tradition and because home canned foods taste great—for example, there isn't a frozen or factory-canned green bean in the world that can match the taste of home canned green beans. I can for the same reasons and include my kids in the ritual.

In my kitchen, I have one of my grandmother's old blue Ball canning jars. Blue jars haven't been made in decades, so of course I don't can with it. I use it as a holder for spatulas and large cooking spoons.

But at the beginning of every canning season, I look at that blue Ball jar and think I have it too easy. So this year, I decided we'd make strawberry jam the old fashioned way— just strawberries and sugar. No fancy store-bought pectin. My grandmothers didn't have that.

When I explain this to my little canning helpers, the 10-year-old says, "but Mom, your granny didn't have the air-conditioning cranked to arctic whenever she canned."

"Yeah. Or an electric stove. Didn't she have to chop wood and can over an open fire?" asks the 12-year-old.

Darned kids. Who knew they were actually listening when I re-told all my grandmothers' stories to them?

"That's not the point," I say impatiently. "The point is we want to experience canning as much as possible like your great and great-great grandmothers did. Without chopping wood, of course. So we're going to make strawberry jam this year with just strawberries and sugar. How hard could that be? This old recipe says to cook the strawberries and sugar rapidly for 40 minutes."

"What does 'rapidly' mean, exactly?" asks the 10-year-old.

"It means 'boil,'" I reply, as if I actually know.

Forty minutes later, I pour thick, blackish stuff that looks like lava and smells like burned strawberries into our eight pint jars. The kids and I stare at the jars.

"I don't think we have to worry about it gelling," says the 12-year-old. "You probably couldn't stick a knife in it."

"Don't be silly," I say, grabbing a spoon and plunging it into one of the jars. The strawberry jam immediately claims the spoon as its own. Within ten seconds, the jam crystallizes into rock hardness around the spoon. I lift the whole jar by the end of the spoon. We all stare at the jar, suspended by the spoon/crystallized strawberries, as if at the result of a bizarre magic trick.

"Umm... what would our great-great-grandmothers say if we tried again with pectin?" the 10-year-old asks quietly.

"That progress is a wonderful thing," I say.

The second batch—made with that fancy store-bought pectin—turned out beautifully.

(June 21, 2004)

~ ♥ ~

'Miss Suzy' Makes the Holiday Brighter

Every year at this time, I hope for that unexpected something that will put the sparkle in my tinsel, the jingle in my voice, the crunch in my peanut brittle.

Sure, I do all the traditional things that are supposed to invoke holiday cheer: listen to carols, munch on cookies, attend services to contemplate the spiritual meaning of the season, and so on. But, I find I always need that unexpected something to put a super-shiny big red bow around my whole holiday season.

Of course, we all know what happens when we try to look for unexpected somethings. We don't see them, because, after all, if we're looking, then we're expecting.

But, frankly, this has been a kind of tough year— illnesses in our extended family (everyone's doing a bit better now, thank you); the rough and tumble of the political year. The usual stresses that go along with juggling family and work and personal needs.

So this season, I made a big mistake; I actively started looking for that unexpected holiday something. At a tree-lighting/caroling ceremony? Nope. In stringing lights across the shrubs? Nope. In placing stockings by the fireplace? Nope, again.

These are all great opportunities for unexpected holiday somethings to pop out, but unexpected somethings do not like to be stalked, and will hide until finally ignored, so they can pop out in their own good time. This is especially true of unexpected holiday somethings.

I'd finally given up and found myself starting to sink into only going through the motions of the holiday when a darling little niece, *Miss Suzy*, and a chance moment at a Santa breakfast all came together to provide my unexpected holiday something.

My mother-in-law treated her in-town kids and their families to breakfast-with-Santa at the lovely Dayton Woman's Club. I sat next to my sister-in-law and we chatted amiably. Then, my niece came over and sat on her mom's lap and somehow or another, the conversation led to squirrels. It seems my sis-in-law and niece find squirrels extra adorable.

My niece, who is three, started talking about why she likes to look at squirrels, her face alight as she spoke. So I told her about one of my favorite childhood books—*Miss Suzy*.

Miss Suzy is a squirrel that lives happily in her tree, until some mean squirrels chase her away. But she finds temporary refuge in a dollhouse in an attic and frees some toy soldiers who have been confined for years to a toy box. The toy soldiers help her reclaim her original home— peaceably, the book says—and Miss Suzy lives happily ever after.

I'm not sure why the book (by Miriam Young) charmed me so as a kid, but it did. Even my butchered re-telling charmed my niece.

I knew I had to find a copy of the book for her. Now, the book was published when I was three and so I held out little hope for finding a copy. But I was surprised to learn that the book is readily available and in its 40th printing (about the same number of "printings" I've gone through since I first had the story read to me.)

So, my unexpected holiday something pleasantly popped up to find me after all. I can't wait to give this book to my niece, the anticipation of which puts the stripes on my candy cane, the cocoa in my mug, and the super-shiny big red bow around my whole holiday season.

(December 13, 2004)

~ ♥ ~

Calendar cover(s) irony

We have a sweet calendar tradition in our family: every year, we pick twelve photos to go on our family calendar. In February, for example, we enjoy looking back at the previous year's Valentine's photo.

And each year, one photo gets the biggest honor of all: being chosen as the calendar's *cover* photo.

Most years, choosing the cover photo has been simple. My husband and I say, "Gee, let's use this really cute picture featuring *both* our daughters for the cover!" And our daughters say, "OK!"

But this year's calendar cover conversation went differently. Like this...

My daughters and I: "Gee, let's use this really cute picture featuring *both* the dog and..."

My husband: "No! No way! Huh uh! Gimme that picture..."

Daughters and I hopped in the car before my husband could grab the picture, and took off for the calendar-making shop. My husband... and the dog... finally stopped chasing us, after about five blocks.

Now, the picture in question is perfectly sweet. It's just a picture of my husband holding our beagle. No big deal, right?

So why did my husband act so horrified at the notion of this photo gracing our 2005 calendar cover? And why did the rest of us get such a kick out of selecting this photo for the 2005 calendar cover?

We'll have to go back in time and work forward for all to become clear.

Twenty-five or so years ago... my then-boyfriend: "I think you should know, before we seriously start dating, that I am not a dog person. Really. Cats are great. Guinea pigs and fish, maybe. But I'm just not a dog person."

Twenty or so years ago... my then just-married-to-me-a-year husband: "I know the litter of puppies we found in the garage [of a house we'd just rented] are all cute. But no, we can't keep even one. We'll have to find homes for them. I am NOT a dog person. Really."

Twelve or so years ago... my husband (who was also a new father): "No, I definitely do not think getting a puppy so 'it can grow up with our children' is a good idea. I am NOT, NOT, NOT a dog person! REALLY!"

Four or so years ago... "OK, sure, it's pitiful that the kids make pretend-dogs out of old milk cartons and drag them around with yarn-leashes. But no, I do not think we should give in and get them a dog. Once and for all, I am REALLY NOT A DOG PERSON! REALLY!"

Eighteen months ago... "What? You say we're getting a dog anyway, despite all these years of me telling you I'm not a dog person? All right... but understand this. I will never be responsible for the dog. I will not ever like the dog. I will only call the dog, 'the dog.' Because I'm REALLY NOT A DOG PERSON AT ALL!"

Two months ago... my husband came home weary from a tough day at work and a long evening of holiday shopping. All he wants is a little comfort, a little understanding. Which my daughters and I were more than willing to offer... except we never got the chance.

My husband scooped up the dog, gave him a hug and said, "Hello there, sweet little doggy, man's best friend! It's so nice to come home to someone who's happy to see me no matter how tough a day I've had..."

I grabbed the camera and captured the moment.

After all, what better calendar cover than a picture of someone who's really, really not a dog person... and his dog?

(January 10, 2005)

~♥~

Staging your home-sweet-home

When selling your house, it is not enough to price it right, keep it in good repair, clean it, and hire a Realtor. No, these days, you must do something called "staging," particularly if you're planning on having an open house.

At least that's what I was told by Internet tips-for-home-seller sites, countless HGTV shows, and several friends keen on interior design, including one who is taking classes in that subject and who assures me that "staging" is indeed a class topic.

My idea of interior design has heretofore been artfully arranging—nay, layering—my kids' creations on the fridge with very cute (and sometimes informative, if from pizza place on corner) magnets. Still, I decided in a hopeful moment to heed everyone's staging advice.

Step one in house "staging" is to remove all the very cute magnets—and all the layers of kiddy art underneath.

The driving philosophy behind "staging" is that you want to create the following fantasy for prospective homebuyers:

This house could be your house. It has never actually been lived in by real people. This is why there are no personal photos or mementos or awards or diplomas on display... so you can imagine yourself in this house...

If you live in this house, you will never have dirty laundry or dishes. Your spouse will never spill his/her morning coffee on the white-carpeted steps, then leave for work without noticing. Your children will each only have three toys, which will be neatly displayed on dust-free shelving units and/or upon beds, which your children will neatly make up without argument.

Your pets will never mess.

Your plants will never droop. In fact, fresh bouquets will spontaneously grace your candlelit dining table.

Your bathroom will be as a spa, and your bed turned back for your comfort and rest, with white sheets free of lint and pet hair.

Of course, anyone creating this staging is laughing hysterically the whole time, knowing no one lives like this, really.

And yet, for our open house, I indulged in staging.

Which meant putting away all personal photos, mementos, etc., buying fresh flowers, turning back beds with brand new white sheets, rolling up brand new white terry cloth towels for display on the bathroom counter—all of which required so much energy that I skipped showers, fed my family at the drive-thru too often, and yelled at the dog more than once.

But our staged home looked great for our open house.

We let our Realtor in and ourselves out and went to someone else's open house... which was also 'staged.'

Ahhh, I thought. I can just imagine myself here. If I live in this house, my kids will make their beds without fuss, the dog will be perfectly neat, my plants won't droop, I'll always have fresh bouquets, and a mint will magically appear on my pillow each night.

Did I hear an echo of the homeowner's hysterical laughter?

Perhaps. But by then, I was too weary from my own staging to worry about it. I breathed the fragrance of the fresh bouquet and thought, "Ah, home sweet stage!
(February 21, 2005)

~♥~

CHAPTER 5

~♥~

Love is a Duct Tape Purse

The curse of the round face... Sweetie

I always thought that when I hit my forties, I'd be appalled at being called Ma'am. Instead, people half my age instead call me Sweetie and in a tone that implies I'm half *their* ages.

At my favorite coffee shop, the barista—inevitably young enough to be my kid—calls me Sweetie. The grocery bag kid calls me Sweetie. Even kids trying to sell me fundraisers... for their junior high sports teams... call me Sweetie.

And so, suddenly, I wanna be Ma'am. I've got the wrinkles and stretch marks to prove I'm old enough to be Ma'am. I've had enough life experiences to earn the title

Ma'am. I think the next time someone calls me Sweetie, I'll scream, "I'm a grown woman! Take me seriously! CALL ME MA'AM!"

But I fear this tactic might backfire. Someone would probably say, "aw, she's so cute when she's mad." The fallout from that would not, however, be cute.

So I decide to work on upgrading my image from Sweetie to MA'AM.

I check my voice: La, la, la, la. OK, it's not because of my voice. I have a rather deep alto voice. And I even use big, grown up words from time to time. For example, "beleaguered." As in, I feel *beleaguered* when strangers who barely have a driving learner's permit feel they have full license to call me Sweetie.

I check my wardrobe: nope, no pinafores, jumpers or super-ruffled blouses. I even wear grown-up leather shoes and boots—not tennis shoes—with jeans.

Then I catch a glimpse of my face in my mirror and find myself reaching to pinch my reflection's cheeks. Aha. It's... THE CURSE OF THE ROUND FACE.

In our culture, round face equals baby face. And baby faces are not taken seriously. Angular, long or chiseled faces are seen as sophisticated.

Let's look at examples from the world of movie stars. NOT ROUND-FACED—Sarah Jessica Parker, Bette Midler, Sandra Bullock, Julia Roberts, Sigourney Weaver, Meryl Streep. ROUND-FACED—um.... Goldie Hawn?

See what I mean?

I want a Weaver-Streep-Roberts face!

However, cosmetic surgery is out of the question. So I do cosmetic research instead and find tips: put a darker slash of blush below the apples of your cheeks! Make up your eyes to draw attention to them! Wear long dangly earrings to make your face look longer! Poof up the crown of your hair!

I then proceed to try all these tips at once and rush back out to my favorite coffee shop, eager to test my new Ma'am look. And... no one calls me Sweetie. But no one calls me Ma'am either. In fact, everyone seems eager to rush me along.

When I go to the lady's rest room, I discover why. I guess I should have checked my look in my home mirror. The blush intended to give me faux cheekbones instead makes me look like an extra in *Night of the Living Dead*. One dangly earring is tangled in my hair, and the other has somehow looped itself up into my ear. And my hair looks like it's formed itself into a bird's nest.

I go home, wash my face, brush my hair... and return to looking like round-faced me. The next time I order coffee out, sure enough... the barista calls me Sweetie.

But I don't flinch this time. I just consider it a sign that I'm putting my best face forward.

(March 14, 2005)

~♥~

Navigating the river of life

I'd forgotten all about my previous experience, until someone asked "have you ever done this before?"

Until that moment, I'd been humming a favorite church song, which partly goes, "Jump in to the river of life…"

But at the question, I stopped humming, contemplated ripping off helmet and life jacket and running back to the rickety bus that had transported our group of wanna-be white water rafters to West Virginia's New River.

The woman asking the question looked nervous, though, so instead I said, "Yes. Don't worry. You'll be fine."

So she got on the big raft with the guide. Suddenly, I wanted to be on the big raft, too. Getting in the two-person kayak with my husband and letting my kids take off in one-person kayaks—no guides on board, except our own wits—no longer seemed like a great idea. But by then, we were paddling down the New River.

I had just enough time, before we hit the first rapid, to remember that first trip from twenty years before, which was actually in inner tubes (not rafts or kayaks). No guide. No helmet. No life jackets. And really, no wits… considering we were inner-tubing down California's Kern River. On an afternoon with river conditions that the Olympic kayaking team deemed too dangerous for practice.

Back to the present trip. We made it just fine through the first rapid and I thought, well, I have learned something, in my trip down the river of life. For one thing, after you've jumped in, it helps to have guidance.

On the literal river, our guide described each rapid and how to best handle it. He said things like "it's best to go into the rapids straight, as counter-intuitive as that might seem. If you go into rapids sideways, you're more likely to capsize."

We followed his advice and capsized in the third rapid anyway.

Which made his other advice—"you're in charge of your own destiny!"—seem not entirely true. After all, we couldn't control what the rapids were like, although we could control how we handled them. Or, at least, how we reacted (pull up your feet! Hang onto the raft! Don't worry about the paddle!) when we couldn't handle them. So I really think his advice should have been, "you're in charge of how you react to your own destiny!"

Once I realized that, I decided to relax and enjoy the trip. It was, after all, going to be 11 miles and 5 hours—a long time to be nervous, even as the family's token wimp.

Which taught me another lesson about both the New River and the river of life: those things that at first make you scream in fear, "Oh, crud!" (or something similar but unprintable) may, after you've developed some experience, become those things that make you gleefully holler "Wheeee!"

On the last rapid, my husband and I almost flipped over a rock we didn't see coming (of course, our kids expertly avoided it). We were so glad to avoid that fate that we didn't pay attention about where to pull in, and accidentally paddled onto the wrong bit of shoreline, then had to get back in the river to catch up with everyone else.

In trying to get back in the boat, we managed to flip out. The locals, watching us from under a tree, were not amused, although physical humor doesn't get any better than that. This time, though, we came up laughing.

Such is the river of life. And I'm glad we jumped in, after all.

(June 20, 2005)

~♥~

Little things can be the most affirming

I am not a big believer in signs, omens or portents. My choices are based on research, planning, and discussions with experts and the other people involved in the decision.

Not only that, but said decision comes with a contingency table that could seat 50, with room left over for china and candles.

Some might say this approach demonstrates a lack of faith in the universe.

I call it pragmatic.

Still…

The last time we moved—after a long flurry of packing/unpacking, cleaning, repairing and painting—I finally one morning found myself feeling a bit wistful. Even a little sad.

Would we, I wondered, be able to hear the sound of the train whistle from our new house?

Maybe that sounds trivial, but for nine years we'd lived close enough to the town's train tracks that I'd become not just used to, but fond of, the sound of the whistle as the freight train rushed through the town's center. We'd moved out to the edge of town, and that morning, I suddenly found myself saddened by the idea of not hearing the train whistle from our new house.

It was a cool morning and I opened the kitchen window to let in fresh air. And promptly heard—albeit a little more faintly—the sound of the freight train's whistle.

The sound made me smile, maybe because it always makes me think of continuity, of life going on. The sound is not a sign or portent or omen, but an affirmation. That life, even after major change, will be OK.

Fast forward six years when, a few months ago, we moved again.

After a long flurry of packing/unpacking, cleaning, repairing and painting, I finally one morning found myself feeling a bit wistful. Even a little sad.

I couldn't quite put my finger on what was bothering me. After all, we'd made our move based on research, planning, and much discussion. We'd analyzed our options and made a sound, pragmatic choice of both house and neighborhood. All the important factors had a tick mark in the "yes" column.

I was pleased with our new house, our new neighborhood. It seemed ungrateful to feel anything except, well, grateful.

Still...

I got a cup of coffee, went out to the back porch, settled down on the porch swing, and tried to figure out what was bothering me.

Finally, I realized what it was. Even with all the planning and contingency tables, I'd forgotten to factor in proximity to trains. At this home, we weren't anywhere near a train track. There was no way I'd hear the sound of a train whistle.

Trivial, I told myself. Go back inside and get to work, I told myself.

But something kept me out on the porch. And after a while I was surprised and delighted to hear the clean pealing of church bells.

I had to smile. The bells rang out from a church that isn't my denomination or where I choose to worship, but no matter.

As the freight train whistle had, the church bells made me think of continuity, of life going on. Not a sign or portent or omen, but an affirmation. That life, even after major change, will be OK.

(August 1, 2005)

~♥~

Ups and downs of people-watching

The most amusing thing about amusement parks is people-watching.

My favorite, yet-to-be-topped moment of amusement park people-watching was several years ago.

My family was at the end of a long roller-coaster line when we observed the following: a group of folks in black leather, tattoos and various metal piercings trooped past us in one direction, paused and stared. We looked to see what had caught the group's attention.

It was another group, this one comprised of "plain-dressed" folks: women in white bonnets, long dresses and aprons; men in black hats, black pants, suspenders, and white shirts.

We overheard someone at the front of the leather/pierced group quietly mutter, in regard to the plain-dressed group, "how strange."

Then the two groups passed and someone at the end of the plain-dressed group stared back at the leather/pierced group and quietly muttered, "how strange."

I've never been able to top that perfect-storm moment of amusement park people-watching, but I keep looking and hoping. In the meantime, here's what I've observed.

For some reason, we hear about road rage and check-out line rage, but we never hear about roller-coaster-line rage. People who will sit in their air-conditioned automobiles, complaining about the five-minute wait at the fast-food or ATM drive-through, will nevertheless docilely wait in heat and humidity for an hour (or longer) for a two-minute thrill ride.

OK, me too.

I also love how people at the end of a roller coaster ride hoot and holler things like, "oh, yeah... we did it! Awesome, man! Woo-hoo!" as if riding a roller coaster is (a) an accomplishment and (b) they are the first people to ever do so. News flash, all ye who hoot and holler thusly: that metal seat designed to look like a super-speedy race car or a fighter jet or a mineshaft car really isn't! It's just a roller coaster!

OK, OK. I hoot and holler thusly, too.

People are at an amusement park to have fun, relax and escape their problems, right? And yet... ever notice that some of the grimmest expressions of humanity can be observed among amusement park attendees? Maybe the expressions are from park entry fee sticker shock. Maybe they're from one funnel cake too many.

I don't *think* I do this. After all, I try to lead my kids in cheery camp songs whenever we're faced with a long ride line. Which might explain *their* grim expressions…

And finally, I've noticed that somehow, every now and then, people who should not be allowed within 100 yards of a basketball court manage to win a basketball in the games section of the amusement park. These same people then try… *try*… to dribble the basketball all around the park. All I can do upon observing this sudden self-delusion of basketball athleticism amongst my fellow amusement-park attendees is mutter "how strange."

And feel pleased with my decorum. After all, I know I don't do that annoying basketball thing!

Although once, upon winning a stuffed pink piggy, I did a victory waltz up and down the midway.

And I think I overheard someone walking past while bouncing a basketball, mutter, "how strange…"
(August 22, 2005)

~♥~

Halloween morphing: cute, scary, no biggie

This Halloween, my 13-year-old is trick-or-treating for what she says will probably be her last outing, and she's rerunning last year's character, Marie Antoinette's ghost, wearing a yellow formal that used to be her grandmother's, and a squiggly line of red food gel around her neck.

My 12-year-old is wearing jeans and a sweatshirt and her father's lion mask, left over from some adult do of a Halloween past. She calls herself "the pre-teen lion mutant."

I guess I should be thrilled. This year, the cost for Halloween costumes in my household was exactly nothing. Unless you count the red food gel.

This year, the effort I had to expend helping my kids get together their costumes was exactly none.

For my first child's first Halloween, I carefully made a pumpkin outfit to wear over her winter coat. Never mind that she wasn't quite two, that her little sister had just been born, that we had a snowstorm that year, or that we were only taking her to three houses.

After all… this was my first chance as a mom to dress up my child for Halloween!

Thus was born a tradition of starting in mid-September to discuss—and fuss—about Halloween costumes.

There was the Halloween I spent too much on Disney outfits. But as my kids dressed up as Belle and Little Mermaid, their grins of joy made me decide the expense was worth it.

There were the Halloweens the kids convinced us we needed to dress up, too. One year my daughters and I were flapper girls, and my husband was a gangster. Another year, we were characters from the *Wizard of Oz*.

But then, sometime along the way, the kids decided it was embarrassing if their parents dressed up. I think that may have been the year I put on a fake beard to be "the bearded lady of the neighborhood" and my husband dressed up as ultra-nerd.

And not long after that, my kids stopped wanting to be cute characters and wanted to be gruesome. How did we go so quickly from fluffy bunny to dead bunny? From Belle in the yellow dress to Marie Antoinette's ghost in the yellow dress and red food gel?

I think that's when I started whining about how expensive and time-consuming Halloween costuming can be.

Halloween costumes weren't mentioned at all this year until a week or so ago, when lion-head-preteen-mutant and Marie-Antoinette-the-ghost assured me they didn't need my help.

That, of course, is the moment I became sentimental about Halloween costumes.

I hope I can remember the lesson learned—enjoy the madness while it lasts—when the next big costuming stage of their lives roll around in a few years, because I have a feeling *that* will be more spine-shivering than even Halloween.

Of course I mean *prom*! What's scarier than a sugared-up two-year-old, a queenly ghost, or a preteen mutant showing up at your door?

Your daughters' prom dates…

Hmmm. Maybe their daddy and I should dress up to answer the door. I think I'll hang on to the bearded lady/ultra nerd costumes.

(October 31, 2005)

~♥~

Lifting a glass of autumn's finest

I stare at the last of this season's apple cider, which I have poured into a wine glass. I've chosen such a fancy glass for what most view as a modest beverage in honor of the cider itself, knowing that once I've imbibed it, I won't have the chance to enjoy cider for another ten months or so.

I contemplate the deep amber color of the cider. I sniff the crisply tangy, yet sweet, aroma. Both color and aroma evoke in my mind's eye the scenery along the drive to the orchard where we always buy cider every fall, the Crossroads Orchard, west of the Miami River, nestled on a country road between Miamisburg and Germantown. I see the trees, turning yellow, orange, red, their colors so brightly beautiful against a sky burnished to a deep blue from a summer's worth of hot days, that it hurts, just a little, to look at them.

Then there's the drive back. We always pause at the top of the hill to stare down at Miamisburg and the church spire and building tops and tree tops and the river and, sometimes, a freight train chugging along on the tracks by the river. Then we drive down the hill and quickly lose our bird's eye view.

But that's OK. We've just experienced autumn the way we most enjoy it—a pretty little country drive to a pretty little country orchard operated by some of the nicest people we've ever met.

We tell ourselves it's just the taste of the cider—unlike the thin, homogenized kind you can get at the grocery—that has inspired us to make this trip, Saturday after Saturday, for about eight or nine weeks each fall, for the past decade.

But secretly we know, it's just as much about the trip itself.

And now I'm contemplating my last glass of the year. I'm reluctant to sip it, because I have some serious questions.

Will I savor the cider? Or gulp it a little too quickly, as I have several times this autumn, thoughtlessly forgetting to enjoy a pleasure that flits in and out of our lives as quickly as the leaves turn brilliant, then scatter in the first frost-tinged wind?

Or should I invest in a freezer, just for cider? You can freeze it, you know. You just pour a little off the top of the bottle, to give the cider room to expand, and then recap it tightly and pop it in the freezer. It's not as crazy as it sounds. People have cellars just for wine. Why not a freezer just for cider? In its own way, the beverage is just as sweet an experience as wine.

I finally take the first sip of my last glass of this year's cider, making sure to savor the sweet, crisp, tart flavor before swallowing.

And the answer to my cider-freezer question is in the taste and aroma and even the amber color of the cider itself.

If I could have cider any time—say, on New Year's Eve, or in the midst of February, or poolside, July 4—then it wouldn't be a treat. It would become just another commodity in a Big Gulp world. I'd forget the lessons that cider teaches me for several quick weeks every fall.

To feel gratitude for those who craft things like cider.

To pause and enjoy the views.

To relish the trip.

To sip.

To savor.

(November 7, 2005)

~♥~

Leaf herding
Now that we live in a house that shares a yard with 12 humongous trees, I've discovered a new fall pursuit that, apparently, many homeowners have been enjoying for some time now.

Leaf herding.

I've always loved fall, though, and so I was thrilled when our huge trees started turning lovely shades of yellow, red, orange. For several mornings in a row, I enjoyed a cup of coffee and the view.

Then one morning, we're all startled from our slumber by a "whump" and a "bzzzzz." We run outside to see what's happening. It turned out that "whump" is the sound of collective leaves falling to the ground, and "bzzzzz" is the monotone chorus of neighborhood leaf blowers.

"We need a leaf blower," my husband says. "I'll go research options…"

"No way," I proclaim. (Keep in mind this was *before* my morning cup of coffee.) "We'll just use good, old-fashioned rakes for good, old-fashioned aerobic, family fun. Shouldn't take more than half an hour, right?"

That evening, all four of us arm ourselves with rakes. As we rake, more leaves fall. A few hours later, it's dark, so two of us aim flashlights to help the two with rakes see to keep raking. We have raked so many leaves to the curb that we have turned the road in front of us into a one-way lane, and still the leaves are falling faster than we can rake.

"Enough," I declare. "Tomorrow morning, we're going to buy a leaf blower."

"Well, if you insist," my husband says. "I'll go do research."

The next afternoon, we have our new leaf blower. I like it because it is red and shiny. My husband likes it because it is electric and made of titanium or something. (He's done his research.)

"This will be great," I say. "It'll just take us a half hour to move all these leaves to the curb!"

Thus, we become leaf herders—for the next two hours. At least this time, though, it's still light when we're done and we survey our green, leaf-free yard with satisfaction. My husband writes me a note. (We can't talk just yet because our ears are still ringing from the leaf blower's "bzzzzz.") The note says: "Same time, next week?" I write back, "sure!"

So we retire for the evening, pleased at how relatively easy this whole leaf herding thing is turning out to be, now that we have a red, shiny titanium leaf blower... until we're awoken the next morning by a loud "whump."

We run to the window and look out. Our yard is again covered in leaves. Not only that, but an even more powerful leaf blower than ours—Mother Nature's overnight windstorm—has blown the leaves from their curbside corral back onto the yard, where they're skittering freely, making little "woo-hoo!" sounds as they trip over one another in an effort to get as far away from the curb as possible.

Out we go, to herd them back to the curb.

Now, the "whump!" (leaves falling), the "bzzzzz!" (us leaf-herding), and the "woo hoo!" (leaves gone wild) has become a daily routine.

Eventually, when all the leaves have fallen and been raked up, I know it will be a real relief.

But deep down, I'm not really looking forward to that moment, because I know this winter I'll look at the bare limbs of our dozen big trees and long for spring—and the first signs of winter re-leaf.

(November 14, 2005)

~❤~

How to get your kids' attention... or maybe not...
Forget being Soccer Mom, Basketball Mom, Band Mom, Working Mom, Stage Mom, or even Super Mom.

I have become something so much more formidable: SPAM MOM!

Some might find this loathsome. After all, spam is the term that describes those annoying emails about get-rich-quick schemes, invigorating body parts that could probably use a rest, and really cheap software.

So what kind of mother would become Spam Mom?

Well, you know all those anecdotal stories about how challenging it is to communicate with your kids in their teen years? Turns out, they're true.

It also turns out that, although teens prefer stony stares or monosyllabic grunts when communicating with parents, they just can't seem to get enough of communicating with their friends. So they ask for things like instant messaging and cell phones and e-mail.

We said "absolutely not" to I-M-ing (as the kids call it) and "later" to cell phones, thus validating our kids' suspicion that we're fuddy-duddies. We said "yes" to email, but only after installing enough anti-spam, who-the-heck-are-you-to-email-my-kid protection blockers to foil even the most determined Internet Houdini.

Shortly thereafter, my gradual metamorphosis into Spam Mom began innocently enough.

For example, my oldest child's social studies teacher sends parents a weekly email about upcoming projects and tests. So I decided to forward those emails to my daughter, after reading them myself.

Then I ran across information about upcoming basketball games that I just knew my youngest would love to have.

Perhaps the lack of "thank you, mom, for those emails" at dinner that night should have been a clue, but still, I persisted.

Then finally came the night when I took the final steps to becoming the creature my kids now fear… Spam Mom.

You see, one of my kids needed a little reassuring about an upcoming test. I did my best, but was still met with stony silence and monosyllabic grunts.

So I decided to reiterate my reassurance to her via e-mail. I admit I became a little carried away, for you see, I wrote a whole "You Can Do It!" motivational lecture.

Which of course I felt my other kid could benefit from, too, so I copied her on the e-mail.

I felt great! After all, I'd just delivered an entire motivational speech without being interrupted, sighed at, or seeing the whites of my kids' eyes!

Spam Mom rules! And why stop there? Sure, let's get IM… but not for Instant Messaging. For Instant Momming! ("r u eating healthy lunch 2-day?" Cell phones? Sure! ("Hi hon. Don't forget to bring home your gym clothes!")

Hold on a sec, while Spam Mom sends a quick e-mail to her kids to let them know the great news that she is expanding her electronic reach into their universes…

I'm back, but it seems I need to rethink my strategy.

Somehow, my kids have figured out how to put Spam Mom on their e-mail blocked list.

(January 16, 2006)

~♥~

Love has no strings—er, duct tape—attached

Love is a duct tape purse.

OK, maybe that doesn't sound as appealing on this Valentine's eve as the more traditional analogies.

And way back when I was in the courting/newlywed stages of my relationship with my husband, I would have been appalled at that statement.

No, I'd have protested, love is romantic music, roses, chocolate, wine!

But now, if I had a time machine and could visit my 20-something self, I'd say: Look, honey. If you're lucky, eventually you'll understand... love is a duct tape purse.

How so?

Well, over the years my husband and I have come to a few understandings about romantic holidays. Sweetest Day we ignore. Valentine's Day we say we'll skip, then give each other a mushy card or a flower anyway. Anniversaries we always celebrate.

But two years ago, my husband surprised me with a most unique Valentine's gift: a duct tape purse! Filled with chocolates. And presented with a heart-warming song.

He knew how much I love purses, so when he ran across a magazine article about duct tape purses, he knew what he had to do: spend four hours crafting mine—a jaunty silver and black striped job, complete with a sturdy base (cardboard covered in duct tape). He knew I'd like the classy stripes, the roominess, the nifty handle. And he knew I'd laugh raucously about such a gift—enjoying the humor in it. Which I did.

Knowing what your partner will find both funny and delightful... that's why love is a duct tape purse.

A few nights later, I wore the purse with a royal blue dress to the opera. My husband was stunned. "You're really going to take the purse?" he asked. But I could tell he was really pleased. And I carried it proudly. I have to admit, when someone would stare at me and my purse, I enjoyed gazing back with an expression that said, "What?"

A few weeks ago, our 12-year-old noticed the duct tape purse on the shelf with all my other purses. Mom, she said, daddy worked really hard on that! And you haven't carried it in a long time.

It was true, and I felt a little sad. I also realized my husband had never whined or complained—hey, I worked hard on that duct tape purse! Why don't you carry it? The choice to wear or not wear my jaunty duct tape purse was entirely up to me—no nagging.

Which is also why love is a duct tape purse. No strings—or, well, duct tape—attached.

So on future Valentine's days, don't be surprised if you see me toting my duct tape purse. It seems like a good Valentine's tradition to me.

After all, I like chocolate, wine, roses and romance as much as any woman.

But I like even better being at a place in life and my marriage where I understand that love is a duct tape purse. (February 13, 2006)

~♥~

A pointed Generation Gap

I always knew the time would come when I'd somehow find myself on the senior side of Generation Gap, with my kids on the junior side of an unbridgeable chasm.

I figured it would be over the usual things: Clothes. Lifestyles. Music. Politics. And that it would happen sometime in my kids' late teens or early 20s.

I sure never thought it would be brought about by writing implements.

It all started the Saturday morning my 14-year-old was scheduled to take a standardized test, the kind wherein the test-taker must carefully color in the oval next to the answer with a No. 2 pencil.

"Have everything you need to get through the test today?" I asked.

"Of course," she said. "Water bottle, hard candy—for quick energy boosts—and two pencils."

"No. 2 pencils?"

"Yeah, I said that—two pencils."

"No, no—do you have two, No. 2 pencils?"

"Yes. I. Have. Two. Pencils." She pulled them out of her backpack.

"Those are mechanical pencils," I said.

"Yeah," she said, drawing out the word into at least three syllables. "That's what everyone uses."

"But you need a No. 2 pencil," I said. "Don't you have one? Or, rather, two?"

She looked confused. I dug through the junk drawer and found a stub of an old No. 2 pencil—fortunately, with the "2" still intact near the eraser. "See the 2? That refers to the hardness of the lead. And the pre-test instructions clearly say you have to use a No. 2 pencil."

"But all I have are mechanical pencils—with 0.7 lead."

I stared at her. The kid had the lead size of a mechanical pencil memorized? I didn't even know she had mechanical pencils, instead of old-fashioned No. 2 pencils—pencils the way God meant pencils to be.

That's what I got for letting her buy her school supplies unsupervised.

She was staring at the No. 2 pencil stub. "That," she said flatly, "is one dorky pencil."

"What?!" I snatched the pencil up as if it were suddenly a precious artifact from my youth—which, actually, it apparently was. "How can you say that? I loved No. 2 pencils as a kid! The smell of pencil shavings at the pencil sharpener…"

"Pencil sharpener? Mom, that's the point of a mechanical pencil. You don't *have* to sharpen it. You just put in new lead."

I stared at her. She stared at me. It was clear that we were not going to understand one another.

We stopped at an office supply store on the way to the test site, and picked up a package of No. 2 pencils. I pointed out that for the price of one skinny pack of mechanical lead refill, one could buy about 200 No. 2 pencils. She was not impressed, although she dutifully took two of them into the test with her.

She gave them back, afterward.

Maybe I can come up with a way to use them, and their 198 buddies, to build a bridge back across Generation Gap.

(March 27, 2006)

~♥~

CHAPTER 6

~❤~

Flaming Birthday Donut o' Doom

Runner's humility rounds corner for first-place finish
We let our kids get involved in sports because we hoped they'd learn—through experience, sweat, wins and losses— the great lessons sports are supposed to teach.

Helping the team. Personal best. Winning graciously. Losing graciously.

Turns out, real-life sports don't come anywhere close to the feel-goodness of sports movies. Our kids' experiences haven't quite lived up to slo-mo finish line crosses (or grand slams, goals, or slam dunks) set to a sound track. That's because people are imperfect and life is gritty.

But leave it to a kid to remind us of just why competitive sports can be a good thing for mind and soul as well as body.

And the story's even better because it's about a kid who's not related to us. Or even on our kid's team. In fact, I don't know this kid's name and probably won't be able, someday, to recognize him on a cereal box.

Our 12-year-old daughter runs cross country. This is a sport that just amazes me—the ultimate nonathlete—because it involves people running. For miles. Voluntarily. With no crazed bears chasing them. And no iced-vanilla-latté stations to stop at along the way.

In fact, no one stops in this sport. They just keep going, going, going, whether fast or slow. Plus everyone cheers on everyone else—boys' team cheers on girls' team, and vice versa; high-schoolers cheer on middle-schoolers, and vice versa.

At a recent cross country meet, while waiting for the girls to run, we watched the middle school boys compete. One boy led the pack. Not by just a little bit. And not for just a while.

Sorry, this isn't an underdog-comes-from-behind story. This kid—we'll call him Zippy—led the entire time, and by a huge distance. In fact, there were sections of the course where Zippy would come around a curve and the rest of us would count to five before we'd see kid number two. Zippy won, by a huge margin.

Twenty or so minutes later, we positioned ourselves to watch our daughter run, when up walks Zippy to talk to some boys from another team. (The boys had gathered to cheer on the girls.) While waiting for the girls' teams to start, a boy said to Zippy, "did you win?"

We figured the boy asking the question had been near the back of the pack and hadn't seen Zippy's impressive victory.

But then Zippy answered: "No, we came in second."

It took us a long moment to take in what we'd just overheard. The obvious answer, to us, to "did you win?" was "you bet I did, and whoo-buddy, by a long shot! Shoulda seen me zipping down that lane, my shoes a-fire, leaving everyone else in the dust…"

But to this 12- or 13 year-old boy, the question, and the answer, was about the team. That moment was the finest example of humility and graciousness I've ever observed in sports of any kind, at any level.

It's almost enough to make me put on some tennis shoes and go jogging.

Even without iced-vanilla-latté stations along the way.
(October 2, 2006)

~♥~

Blessings abound if attitude doesn't confound

Find the blessing!

That's a phrase that popped up recently in the middle of my thoughts. Well, in the middle, really, of some internal whining that went something like this: "oh my gosh I have so much chauffeuring to do and errands to run and as for dinner, would pizza two nights in a row really be awful?"

You know the drone. We've all done it—found ourselves pre-occupied by the minutia of daily life, stressed by it, pulled down by it. Media reports abound about the stresses of modern life.

When I realize I'm caught up in that mental swirl, I usually cajole myself with a mental "stop whining!" Which doesn't work in the long term, and so I feel even guiltier the next time I'm caught in the swirl.

But the other day, this little phrase sauntered up, nudged drill-sergeant-stop-whining out of the way, tapped me on the shoulder, grinned at me when I whirled around, and cheerfully hollered, "Find the blessing!"

I'm not sure where the phrase came from, but with Thanksgiving approaching, it seemed appropriately timed, and so I put it to work, something like this:

- Need to get kid A to practice X and kid B to practice Y. At opposite ends of town. At the same time. Find the blessing: they're healthy and active and in positive activities.

- My office is a mess... again. Find the blessing: I have work to do... that's why there's a mess!
- Dinner is running late. Find the blessing: We have plenty of nutritious food. So what if it's on the table 15 minutes later than usual?

For a whole day and a half, that mantra—"Find the blessing!" lightened my mood, refreshed my perspective.

But then I started questioning the concept. After all, cheery mantras have made me sneer in the past—"work smarter, not harder!"—because they always seemed to be applied as a sort of cover up for real issues. What if you can't work smarter, because the required resources aren't available?

What if, damn it, you just aren't in the mood to "find the blessing" because the stress really is just too overwhelming to be patched up with a simple phrase? Because a loss—perhaps of a goal, or a loved one, or a relationship—is really just plain old heart breaking? Because there are real problems that need real solutions above and beyond a glib "'ell, it could be worse" band-aid?

I had to think about those questions for a while, knowing I'd have to find some answers if "find-the-blessing" was going to go beyond glib and really work for me as a way to keep life in perspective.

Here's what I finally came up with. Those questions are good ones. And the answers are: feel the pain, the hurt, the loss as much and as long as needed. Rant and rage at the injustice of the problem.

But then... when all that burns itself out... and it will... there will be a momentary emptiness that will have to be filled with something because the spirit, like nature, abhors a vacuum.

That's when there's a choice—to hang on to whininess or bitterness or stress or loss—or... to find-the-blessing. Not as an end to itself. But as a starting point, perhaps, for deeper solutions.

And sometimes, find-the-blessing may take a long, long time. Maybe, eventually, it will simply be fond memories. Or maybe in the face of much smaller concerns—like the ones that somehow brought the phrase to my mind in the first place—it will help snap things almost immediately into big-picture-perspective.

In any case, may you find lots of blessings.

(November 20, 2007)

~♥~

Let's talk turkey (not!)

'Tis the season of TV holiday specials... you know, Grinch, Frosty, Rudolph, and Charlie Brown... shows our kids always looked forward to with childish glee and joy.

So just a few nights ago, we're not surprised when our progeny cheerfully decide to treat themselves to viewing holiday TV shows. We think this is a fine idea. After all, their homework and chores are done, there's still an hour before bedtime, and we long ago blocked cable channels that could mentally warp our young 'uns.

So, down they go to the family room to croon along with the Peanuts gang to *Christmas Time is Here!* or observe the Grinch's heart grow with the spirit of love.

We decide to treat them to a snack to enjoy whilst watching holiday TV specials, and ponder the options. We know! We'll use up the last of the turkey leftovers for yummy sandwiches!

But before we can get out the bread and the mayo, a commercial break takes place. We hear the pitter-patter of little... well, more like the clomp, clomp of medium-sized... feet coming up the stairs. My beloved and I smile at each other. Aw, won't our kids be thrilled that we're being so nice to them? Won't this be a mega Hallmark/Norman Rockwell family moment in which...

Teen 1: "Did you know that turkeys are genetically engineered to have more white meat?"

Me, pointing to sandwich fixings: "Makes for better leftover sandwiches, so—"

Teen 2: "But that stinks for those of us who like dark meat more!"

Husband, sadly eying the turkey drumstick he's holding, which he'd nabbed for his snack: "Ah, well, it's good that we have this luscious drumstick leftover, then—"

Teen 2: "No, it's not! Genetic engineering is... is... turkey abuse! And so is..."

Teen 1: "The fact that turkeys are kept in cramped quarters and are artificially inseminated..."

Teen 2: "Ew! Gross!"

Teen 1: "...to make more eggs—and thus more baby turkeys—than nature intended."

Me: "Um, ok, well, maybe we should just get a free-range turkey next year..."

Cosmo (the dog), eying the turkey drumstick now drooping in my husband's hand: "Rowr-ow-ow-rowr-awoooo!"

Teen 1: "Why should we have turkey at all? It's just a myth that Ben Franklin wanted the turkey as the national bird, or that turkey was at the first Thanksgiving—I mean, some kind of fowl was consumed, but even if it was a turkey, it was a wild turkey, not one like we've always been told..."

Teen 2: "...is the traditional main course, by the establishment which has been hiding the truth all along."

Teens: glare at us (the establishment) in unison.

Parents: stunned silence. What vile channel's show has transformed our cranberry-cheeked, wholesome children into holiday-tradition protesting, angst-ridden teens?

Cosmo breaks the silence: "Rowr-ow-ow-rowr-awoooo!"

Finally, I say: "What in the world are you watching down there anyway? Some bizarre variation of Grinch, Rudolph, Frosty or Charlie Brown?" I have visions of a warped remix of holiday classics on, say, MTV. Or maybe a whole new holiday special I haven't yet heard about, developed by, say, the creators of South Park.

I also have visions of future Thanksgivings and Christmases, in which my teen daughters will wear black veils and say a memorial over the holiday turkeys and hams.

So I'm about to give them a lecture about making better TV-viewing choices, when...

Teen 1: "Oh, it's an educational show called 'American Eats.'"

Teen 2: "Yeah. On the History channel."

Hmph. I'm renaming it the Grinch channel. Well, at least the dog's happy. He gets the rest of the turkey. Wonder if he'll watch Rudolph, Frosty or Charlie Brown with my husband and me this season?

(December 4, 2006)

~♥~

Tree-skirt tradition captures the fabric of life

I'm not sure who came up with the idea for our home-made Christmas tree skirt--a memory lapse that is not surprising, given that the tradition began 16 years ago.

And every year I wonder: why *did* we decide to use a big circle of red felt as the basis for the skirt? Felt is not exactly the most durable or washable of fabrics. Maybe it had something to do with economics; we started the skirt in 1990, the year we bought our first house.

Or maybe—just as likely—it was because we were craft challenged. (For the record, we still are.)

In any case, in 1990 we started our tree skirt tradition: craft an image from felt and/or fabric paint to commemorate the year nearly past, and add it to the tree skirt.

And so in 1990, we cut out and glued on a blue felt house, with a green felt lawn, and white felt windows.

1991 is Big Ben, representing our trip to Great Britain. 1992 is a rattle, representing our first born.

If you'd asked us in 1990, we'd have told you that 1993 would be another house, since we just knew we'd only stay in our starter house for three years. (We stayed for nine.) But instead we have another, much better, image: another rattle.

Some years have predictable images, such as school buses for when our daughters started school.

Some images commemorate happy surprises—my first published book. (Never thought that would happen!) Getting our dog. (Never thought that would happen, either!)

Some images now seem a little bittersweet, such as the house nine years into our skirt, representing what we thought would be our home forever and always.

But we've learned a few things since starting this Christmas tree skirt tradition. Life isn't predictable. Change is inevitable—a fact that sometimes is frightening, sometimes joyous. And sometimes humorous.

How else to explain the *white* lobster for 2004? You see, we couldn't have known back in 1990 that 14 years later we'd have such a wonderful vacation in Maine that we'd want to commemorate it on our tree skirt with a lobster. But, of course, a red lobster wouldn't exactly show up on a red skirt. So we cut a lobster out of a scrap of white felt, and merrily glued it on.

Last year, the images on our Christmas tree skirt came full circle. We were all sad, not wanting our tradition to end just because we ran out of room.

So, we decided we'd just start a second row above the first. I know that's not the most logical approach to design, but then it does humorously underscore one of the tree skirt's life lessons about plans changing and life throwing curves.

As I write this, we haven't yet decided on the image that will kick off the second row. How best to commemorate Short family life in 2006 on our quirky tree skirt?

But I do know, whatever we choose, that by the time this column appears on Christmas morning, our tree skirt will be snugly tucked around our tree, its figurative love and grace underlying everything else, just as our love for one another is the foundation for all the funny, scary, joyous unpredictable things that life brings us.

And that is my wish for you and yours this Christmas morning: a foundation of love and grace underlying all else life brings.

(December 25, 2006)

~ ♥ ~

Up in smoke! Sweet life lesson all that is left on a plate after birthday mishap

I hadn't planned on sharing this story in print. After all, some private events—however touching, hilarious, or dramatic—just don't need to be column fodder.

But the true star of the story, our 15-year-old, recently said: You are going to write about this aren't you? And then gave me the best reason why I should (which is at the end of the column. No peeking!).

Let's start at the beginning. My daughter and I have birthdays just four days apart. And as much as we love birthday cake, two full-size cakes in the same week is just one cake too many.

So, we've had varying solutions, depending on the year. Two small cakes. Or cake for her and birthday bagels for me (if I'm in a post-holiday dieting phase) or donuts (if I'm not.)

A few weeks ago, the choice was birthday cake for her and birthday donuts for me. With chocolate icing. And cream filling. (Obviously, this isn't a post-holiday dieting year.)

My birthday fell mid-week, so we decided to save the traditional festivities for the end of the day. That evening, as my husband and I were leaving to pick up Younger Daughter from basketball practice, he whispered something to Older Daughter.

Twenty or so minutes later, we returned. I started to open the door from the garage to the kitchen—and it was promptly slammed shut. Younger Daughter asked aloud what we were all thinking: "Is that the smell of... something burning?"

We opened the door again and rushed in. By now Older Daughter was desperately trying to throw something away... except... it was fused to a plate.

And finally, we saw it... my birthday donut. Older Daughter tearfully explained: "I had the big number 4 candle in the middle of the donut and three little candles on each side of the four. It looked like tiara when I first lit it! I went to do homework, and the next thing I knew, I smelled something burning, and... and... the donut was... IN FLAMES!"

We all stared silently at the donut—now a fusion of chocolate icing, dough, candles, candle holder, and plate.

Finally, my husband said, "um, sweetie, I said to put in the candles ... not light them."

Older Daughter: "But I wanted Mom to see it lit as soon as she walked in! I wanted it to be perfect. So I lit the candles... about ten minutes ago."

It was at that point that I burst into laughter.

I mean, really. You hear jokes about getting so old your birthday cake goes up in flames. But my cake... albeit a small one... actually did.

Finally, we were all laughing, making jokes about the scenario, and taking photos of the charred donut. When we finished laughing ourselves silly, Older Daughter got out another donut, stuck in a candle, lit it, and I made a wish and blew out the candle—fast.

A few days ago, she asked if I was planning on writing about what we've since dubbed "The Flaming Birthday Donut of Doom."

Oh, no, I said.

You should, she said.

Why? I asked, horrified at the thought of embarrassing her.

Because it's a funny story, she said.

Stories can't just be funny, I said; they also have to have a point.

But this story does have a point, she said. It's not just about your birthday donut catching fire... it's about trying to make something perfect, and the whole thing going up in flames, but it turning out OK anyway. Maybe even better than what you'd planned.

Ah.

I don't really remember what I wished for when I blew out the candles on the second birthday donut.

But I don't think it matters. After all, what more can a mom wish for than a kid who sees the humor—and the life lesson—in a Flaming Birthday Donut of Doom?

(January 22, 2007)

~♥~

Diary of Snow Days

Snow Day One.

Dear Diary,

What a delightful day with the children. School was cancelled due to a snow day—well, really, a bitter cold day, with a wind chill temperature of negative 20. Brrrr!

I made scrambled eggs and cinnamon toast for breakfast; a rare treat on weekday mornings, since we're usually so rushed.

One of the benefits of self-employment is getting to take a snow day with my darling progeny! So, after breakfast, we all cuddled up in front of a blazing fire in the family room fireplace, read books, and played many games of Yahtzee, Uno, and Backgammon. Then we had hot chocolate. Even the cats and dog curled up at our feet. So cozy!

I'm so glad I took the day off to share with my beautiful offspring, as I'm sure tomorrow it will be warm enough for school to resume.

Snow Day Two.

Dear Diary,

What a surprise! A second day of school cancelled, again due to cold weather.

Warmed up left-over scrambled eggs and cinnamon toast for the children. They complained that the food was rubbery, but I patiently pointed out that elsewhere are plenty of children who would love a warm breakfast, however rubbery.

One can only take off so many days, even if self-employed, so I tried to work. Notice the word "tried." With one kid watching TV, and the other listening to the radio, it was difficult to concentrate.

So I suggested the kids play Yahtzee and Backgammon and Uno again, just the two of them, while mom worked. Well, I tried to work—but I had to stop a few times to interpret rules.

No fire in the fireplace today, although I did light a candle and say a prayer.

The cats and dog are hiding.

Ah well. It's supposed to warm up tomorrow.

Snow Day Three.

Dear Diary,

Yeah, it's another !#$% snow day. This time because it really did snow.

Told the little rug rats they could scrounge up their own blasted breakfast; what am I—their personal chef?

So they arm wrestled for the last piece of leftover cinnamon toast, and the dog came out of hiding to eat the last of the rubbery eggs. Haven't seen cats.

Suggested to spouse that perhaps the kids should go see where daddy works. I guess he didn't hear me through his ear muffs, since he didn't respond… but he did look panicked as he ran out the door.

Thought I might have a few moments peace when the urchins got out Yahtzee, Uno and Backgammon on their own. But no. Who knew there were combat variations of these games?

Am considering applying for jobs that would force me to work outside my home office. Perhaps in Hawaii.

Heard a rumor we might get more snow flurries.

So instead of lighting fire or candles, I'm lighting a heat lamp and running all over town with it. Plus, I'm buying out the grocery's salt supply and sprinkling it on the roads myself.

<u>Not A Snow Day.</u>

Dear Diary,

It warmed up to a balmy 20-some degrees above zero! School is in session!

The peace and quiet is astounding. I can get back to work.

Except… I think instead I might go see a counselor.

Because, truth be told, I miss my darling progeny and am counting the days until spring break.

(February 12, 2007)

~♥~

Mirror, mirror on the wall—*where are my lips?*

Now that I'm officially middle-aged, I have one pressing question.

Where are my lips?

Just a little while ago when I was a teen, I figured that if I lived all those incredibly numerous years into my 40s, I'd have answers to all the major questions—what's the purpose of life? Why are we here? etc., etc.—and would have discovered some new questions.

Well, I'm still not an expert-in-life (although I'm pretty sure the answers to those questions have to do with life is important for its own sake and we're here to love one another) and the only new question I have is…

Where are my lips?

As recently as age 39 I was in full possession of my lips.

There they were—the top lip a little thin, the bottom a little full, both cherry-ish in color, and more or less centered below my nose.

And then… they just started to fade away.

I took vitamins.

My lips kept fading.

I gave my lips lectures, staring in the mirror at the part of my image where my lips used to be, and commanding: "No more lipping off!"

My lips remained pale, so I tried biting my lips (like I did when I was a teen and actually *wanted* to wear lipstick, but wasn't allowed) but that just hurt and didn't bring any color to my lips.

So, finally, I tossed aside my trusty lip balm for tinted lip balm.

My lips came back, for a little while, but soon even the tinted balm wasn't doing the job.

I really didn't want to start wearing lipstick, because I just wanted my lips to stick, not have to keep up with lip makeup maintenance.

But I was getting tired of people asking me if I'd just recovered from the flu—concerns based on lip pallor—and finally decided to put my money where my mouth is. Or was.

Anyway, equipped with several trusty lipstick hues—Magical Merlot and Winsome Wine and Ricocheting Rose—I finally again had a semblance of lips.

Except the lipstick didn't stick just to my lips. It stuck to everything else, too. If lost, I could easily have been tracked by the lip phantoms I left everywhere: on napkins, glasses, mugs.

So I'm back to being the woman with no lips and wondering how that happened.

And please, don't give me any lip about how this isn't exactly a major issue given the state of the world.

Read my lips (if you can): I know this.

Because my lips taking off have given my eyebrows ideas.

And now I have another pressing question.

Where are my eyebrows?

(February 26, 2007)

~♥~

Days of denim conformity long gone

I remember when jeans were easy to wear.

No, I'm not just talking in terms of *physically* easy to pull on, zip up, and button.

Once upon a time, jeans were *mentally* easy to wear, too. You put 'em on simply to relax.

Ah, the good old days. After a week of wearing skirts, suit jackets, and pantyhose, it was so nice to schlep about in weekend wear: jeans and a sweatshirt. Or jeans and a T-shirt.

Then, someone decided to ruin a perfectly good idea—jeans as weekend wear—by instituting "business-casual Fridays." At first, that meant khakis—not jeans. But then business casual crept into the other days of the week, and so of course jeans started being acceptable more and more places.

Now they're everywhere, even on people who a decade or so ago would never have appeared formally in public in them: news reporters, political candidates, business leaders, and so on.

Let's face it: jeans have taken over our closets and our brains.

Sure, we all pretend that, yeah, we're just wearing jeans because we're so into being casual, being real, being laid back.

But the truth is, jeans are anything but casual, real or laid back these days.

In fact, they're downright tyrannical.

Think about it.

Go to a clothing store and try, just try, to find some pants that aren't jeans.

Oh, sure, there are still some suit pants and khakis, but really, they're just shoved on a corner rack, drowning in a denim sea, there to trick you into thinking you're actually opting for jeans because they're oh-so-comfortable.

But jeans don't rule over us by giving us no choices. No, the days of delightful denim conformity are long gone—you know, when your jeans looked like everyone else's jeans except maybe longer/shorter or wider/narrower.

Now we need spreadsheets to keep track of all the options in rises (low, mid, high); washes (light, dark, acid); and cut (boot, straight-leg, bell).

Not only that, but long, serious consideration must be given to exactly what you're communicating with your jeans.

If my jeans are too low-rise, I might be guilty of not only a muffin-top (ugh!) but also of clinging too hard to my youth.

But if they're too high-rise, I'm verging on fuddy-duddy territory.

Dark wash jeans are more formal, and thus seem favored by women at or near my age, paired with a casual jacket and boots.

Pale jeans and sneakers? At my age, that's just for walking the dog.

Rips in jeans? No way. That's for my kids, although I refuse to pay for pre-ripped jeans. I'm still trying to get over the time I was out with my daughter, and just as I noticed in horror a rip in her jeans' knees, another pre-teen wandered by, eyed what I thought of as unseemly tears in my daughter's clothing, and said admiringly: "Great rips!"

I thought the tyranny of jeans had gone as far as it could, but then a few days ago I ran across this report on The Early Show: Remember the colored jeans from the 1980s? Well, they're set to make a comeback. That's right. Blue is out. Red, teal... even yellow jeans are in.

Forget my sentimentality about the good old days of having just a pair or two of weekend jeans, when people ruled jeans, and not the other way around.

The idea of yellow jeans is almost enough to make me sentimental for pantyhose.

(March 26, 2007)

~♥~

Cedar-tree slice evokes Memorial Day memories

Most of the items that decorate the walls in our home are pretty self explanatory: family photos in most every room; framed book covers in my office; candles and vases, here and there.

But one item on the living room wall always gets puzzled looks and requires explanation.

It's an odd-shaped slice from a cedar tree trunk. The slice looks just like a single open quote mark. Its center whorls are dark umber, while the edges near the rough bark are amber.

The slice is from a cedar tree that once stood at the center of a small cemetery near a small village in a small holler in eastern Kentucky, where my family of origin is from. The kind of small, family cemetery that's tended by local farm families, even if none of their kin are buried there.

My maternal grandparents are buried there, and some great-grandparents, and a favorite cousin who died far too young.

As a kid, I knew Memorial weekends were reserved for "visiting the graves," as we called it. We'd go to that cemetery, where a preacher would hold a service, and we'd sing a few hymns, and then leave flowers on the graves, before going on to visit other nearby graves.

Truth be told, my favorite part was taking refuge under the ancient cedar tree. I liked standing with my back against that old tree. There was something sturdy and peaceful about it... comforting... because sometimes what the preacher had to say was kind of scary (at least to a kid), or sometimes the service went on a bit, or sometimes the raw emotion that the hymns evoked was just a little overwhelming.

Those annual treks to visit the graves (and, in my mind, the cedar tree) became semi-annual after awhile, as time passed and the tradition started to fade. Semi-annual morphed into rare... and now it's been more than ten years since I've gone.

Not long after my last visit, I learned from my father that the cedar tree had died, and the cemetery caretakers had put out the word that they had to cut down the tree, for safety reasons. But kin of those laid to rest in that cemetery were welcome to a slice of the tree's trunk.

I jumped at the chance. I got the slice a few weeks later and sanded its surfaces smooth, while being careful not to disturb the bark. Next, I applied a clear coat of varnish to protect the wood.

Then, I hung it in the living room of our first house.

I hung it in the living room of our second house.

Now it hangs in the living room of this home.

And it will be with me wherever we live next.

Usually, I don't give this unique wall decoration more than a passing glance. But though the visiting-the-graves tradition ended long ago, on each Memorial Day, I take a few moments to really look at that cedar slice.

I like remembering how the cedar tree spread its sheltering, comforting branches over all of us gathered at the cemetery for our annual Memorial Day rite.

The tree, back then, somehow conveyed to me in a way the preacher's words didn't that while death brings sorrow, life finds a way of going forward, from one generation to the next, wherever there is love and comfort and compassion.

And I like contemplating how, in its new life as an open-quote-mark shaped decoration, that cedar tree continues to whisper the same message to me.

(May 28, 2007)

~♥~

Between a choice and a high place

While on vacation in Siesta Key, Florida, I vowed that I wouldn't go parasailing with my husband and daughters; I would simply go along for the boat ride and take photographs of them 350-feet aloft in the air.

I made this vow because I am the official family wimp. My husband and daughters seem, to me, fearless about physical activity, whereas I'm always the cautious one. I would be quite comfy with my role as official family wimp, except my family gets annoyed when I call myself that and proclaim that I am not nearly as wimpy as I, well, assert.

I am, in particular, wimpy about water activities (at best I can swim on my back in a pool) and I'm fearful of open heights. (Although, for some reason, I'm fine with enclosed heights such as airplanes and fancy glass elevators in hotels.)

That's why parasailing seemed like a particularly bad idea for me—350 or so feet aloft in a harness clipped to a parachute, tethered to a boat by a cable, over the ocean. No, no thank you.

So I boarded the boat, clutching my camera and bag, releasing my hold only to spritz my family with SPF30, while firmly avowing to the deck hand that no, I would not parasail.

At which point she looked at my husband and two children and said: "Fine. So the two girls will go up first in tandem. And then you, sir. Except you need a partner. So which daughter will go up for a second parasail ride with you?"

My husband and daughters all looked at each other. And then they looked at me.

And I realized I was expected to make the decision: which daughter gets the second parasail ride?

My future flashed before my eyes. I saw clearly that no matter how I made the choice—picking the younger one because parasailing was her idea in the first place, picking the older one because she's older, flipping coins, thinking of a number 1-10—I was doomed.

For the next 40 years--at Thanksgivings and Christmases and all family gatherings future—I'd overhear: "Yeah, well, mom chose YOU to go parasailing a second time!"

All our effort to minimize sibling rivalry and promote family harmony was about to be undone in a matter of seconds, no matter my choice or the logic behind it.

So I made the only possible choice: "I've changed my mind. I'm going parasailing beside my husband."

What mother wouldn't opt for making a complete fool of herself by shrieking and freaking out in fear of water/heights rather than forevermore hearing "Remember that vacation when you chose HER to go parasailing a second time? Always knew you liked her more!"

To their credit, my daughters (who'd said all along I should go) were pleased by my decision rather than squabbling about a second ride.

So that's how I ended up parasailing, something I swore I'd never, ever do.

And, surprise, it was wonderful. Beautiful. Peaceful. Easy. I did not freak out or shriek. I completely enjoyed the experience and I've been enthusing about it ever since to anyone who'll listen.

So I guess my family's right. I'm not such a wimp after all. Or maybe being a mom has made me tougher than I realize.

In any case, I would go parasailing again without hesitation.

On the other hand, if my nutty family members ever want to go parachuting, they're on their own.

Really.

(June 25, 2007)

~♥~

CHAPTER 7

~♥~

Hot Flashes and Gourmet Tomatoes

It's time to give idea of a power nap a rest

Last week, my 13-year-old was eager to embark on her back-to-school shopping, before, she said, all the cute stuff was gone. So, off we went to the store.

Now, school supply shopping with an eighth-grader is vastly different than shopping with, say, a first grader.

With a first grader, you can say, "Look, hon, safety scissors! How about the purple-handled pair?" It's a joyous moment in the annual back-to-school ritual.

With an eighth grader, saying, "Look, hon, folders! How about the one with the cute puppy picture?" —will result in a glare so cold that your brains will freeze.

The best strategy for school-supply shopping with a teenager is to start looking through the supplies yourself, for items you can use, as if you just coincidentally happened across the school-supply area at the same time as your kid. Which is exactly what I did. I picked up pens, trying to project, through Method Acting techniques, that these were for my home office, and would not be pilfered a few months later by the nearby teenager who happened to look like me. Likewise, I selected notepads.

And then I saw it.

The perfect item in the back-to-school section for a 40-something woman like me.

A nap mat.

Yes, the very nap mats used in Kindergarten classes.

It looked so comfy, so tempting. Why, after my kids really *are* back to school, I could whip out my very own nap mat in the middle of the day, and curl up in my office for a little snooze. I was suddenly sentimental for the days—mine, not my kids'—when naps, followed by milk and cookies, were a regular part of the routine. (Of course, I'd call it power napping/snacking for boosting productivity.)

But by then, my eighth-grader was walking away from the back-to-school display, her cart overflowing with cute supplies, and heading for the check out.

After we returned home, I found myself still thinking about that nap mat, and that maybe I should go back and buy it. After all, it was a shade of blue that would coordinate beautifully with my home office décor.

Then a wiser voice whispered in my mind: it's been a long time since you've napped. Think you still can? Before spending hard-earned bucks on a nap mat, why don't you try a power nap on the couch?

So I set a kitchen timer for 20 minutes and curled up.

The first two minutes passed peacefully, and I was just starting to drift off...when the washing machine started thumping as if possessed by sneakers, which it was.

Five minutes later, after readjusting the machine, I was just starting to drift off again...when our beagle started baying at the mail man.

Two minutes later, after collecting the mail, I was just starting to drift off again...when the telephone rang.

Seven minutes later, after a quick conversation, I was just starting to drift off again...when the cat jumped on me.

Four minutes later, after detangling my hair from the cat—or perhaps vice-versa—I was just starting to drift off again...when the kitchen timer buzzed, indicating the end of my 20-minute power "nap."

I headed back to the store. No, not for a nap mat. Obviously, that would be a waste of money.

For the post-nap milk and cookies.

Some childhood comforts should never be given up.
(July 30, 2007)

~ ♥ ~

Having taller kids height of indignity

Every so often, someone says to me: hey, I know a great topic for your column! Why don't you write about…

Somehow, this rarely works out, even if I think the suggested topic is a superb idea.

But this week I'm writing about a topic suggested by my daughters: the fact that they're both taller than I am.

I can't even say I was convinced when they looked up at me with their big, blue and brown eyes, because of course as they made the suggestion, they were looking *down* at me with their big blue and brown eyes.

And grinning gleefully.

Now, I always knew the day would come when my daughters would be taller than I am. After all, my husband is seven inches taller than I am, and kids tend to end up, height-wise, somewhere between their parents.

But as with most milestones in parenthood, I wasn't quite prepared when it happened.

Truth be told, it doesn't seem so long ago that I had to retrieve their mittens off the top shelf of the coat closet, because they couldn't reach them.

Now, I find myself asking them to get cans from the top shelf in the kitchen cabinet so I don't have to get out the step-stool to do it myself.

When I start to look straight across at one of my daughters and find I have to adjust my gaze upward to look her in the eyes, I can have no doubts that my little girls are growing into young women.

I have a friend who advises against getting all sentimental and mushy and weepy about these sorts of things. After all, she asks, what would cause nature to not take its course? Nothing pleasant comes to mind.

She's got a point, but I still indulge in moments of "dang, why'd they have to grow up so fast," especially when, in the process of retrieving for me those cans from the top shelf, my taller daughters also discover my secret M&M's stash.

Still, such moments of sentimentality are coming less often, thanks to my daughters themselves, who are having way too much fun with the fact they're both taller than I.

They now have the Randy Newman hit of old, "Short People" on their iPods and love to sing along to it.

When I try to give a stern lecture that the song is about seeing all people as equal, they just grin down at me and say, "What? Can't quite hear you from up here!"

They take turns leaning on my shoulder, just to point out the height discrepancy.

The other day, we were posing for a photo. My daughters thought it would be fun if we lined up like Cingular bars, a la the Cingular cell phone ads... with me, of course, as the shortest bar.

And it doesn't help that just as my daughters have reached the age for growth spurts, I've reached the age where I've given up high heels for much more sensible (and less painful) flats.

What can I do? Just smile up at them and say: "Stand tall and proud, girls!"

It's not just what I should do as a mother.

Doing so is my only hope of getting back my M&M's stash...

(September 17, 2007)

~♥~

Teen's shiner gleams as a source of pride

My 14-year-old daughter came home from a basketball scrimmage a few weeks ago with a black eye.

My initial reaction: get her an ice pack; hover and coo, "oh, you poor baby! Why didn't you call me right away?" —and suggest signing her up for a more relaxing, and less bruising, activity such as knitting.

Her reaction: point out that her coach had provided an ice pack; explain that she didn't call because doing so wasn't necessary; and remind me that once-upon-a-time I did give her knitting needles and then almost immediately took them away, because she hated trying to knit and instead started chasing her sister with the needles.

After my daughter calmed me down, she explained how she got her black eye. It had something to do with her going for the ball, and an opposing player also going for the ball, and an accidental meeting of hand-and-eye.

Truthfully, I didn't follow the details, because I was busy worrying about her black eye and, at the same time, thinking how when I was her age, my only experience with basketball was conniving my way out of a gym class tournament by convincing the teacher that I really needed to do an article on it for the school newspaper.

After my daughter finished her story, I ran off to the bathroom and emerged a few seconds later with tubes of cover-up and bottles of makeup.

My daughter looked appalled. "Are you kidding? I'm not covering this up!" she said, pointing proudly at her black eye.

But, I said, you'll be teased. Kids will ask you about your black eye! I would have been mortified!

She rolled her eyes at me, proving that getting a black eye doesn't have a negative impact on this absolutely essential teenage-girl communication technique.

However, after Saturday morning's basketball practice, she tried to reassure me by reporting that one of her teammates stared at her black eye and sighed: "I've always wanted a black eye," then closed her eyes, leaned forward and said, "Pop me one. C'mon, just pop me one!" (Of course, none of her teammates complied.)

That story made me laugh, I admit. But then I started worrying about how kids outside the team would react, and how my daughter would feel about that.

So, after school the next Monday, my daughter reported the following conversation between herself and a male classmate:

Him—basketball?

Her—Yeah.

Him (appreciatively)—Yeaahhhh!

She thought that was hilarious.

Now, I've never wanted my daughters to be Mini-Me's. But every now and then something happens—like the Great-Eighth-Grade-Basketball-Black-Eye-Incident, as we've now tagged the story—that really demonstrates how different my daughters are from me.

That's not just based on my reaction as a mother--of course a mom is likely to be fussier over their kids' injuries than the kids are. It's based on knowing how completely differently I would have reacted to the event, had I been in her basketball shoes.

Which, of course, I also can't imagine.

What's a mother to do? Just smile. And maybe look for those knitting needles. Some days, I could use a more relaxing, and less bruising, activity than parenting.

(November 26, 2007)

~♥~

Joy of season rather unseasonal: December fireworks

A few evenings ago, my family and I went out for dinner after a long Saturday of errands, chores, and activities. Not particularly remarkable, until our drive home.

Were those fireworks that we saw in the pitch dark sky?

On a bitterly cold Saturday night in December?

We quadruple-checked amongst ourselves and confirmed we really were seeing fireworks in December. And not just pretty-good-for-a-backyard-launch fireworks.

A real, July-4-worthy fireworks display—only five months late, or seven months early, depending on how you like to look at things.

Now, as I mentioned, we'd all had a long day. And all we'd planned on doing after dinner was to go home and turn in early, since the next day promised to be busy, too.

But, suddenly, there were fireworks in the December sky, and our kids—for all their teenage posturing about being nearly grown-up—sounded just like they had as little girls, saying "Don't go home yet! Find the fireworks' location! Please, please, please, Mom and Dad?"

OK, that got us. It's been awhile since our kids said "please, please, please," in the manner of children.

So instead of turning right, toward home, my husband turned left, toward the fireworks.

A minute or so later, we found the source of the fireworks: someone was setting them off in a huge, wide yard. We pulled off the side of the road within yards of the fireworks' set-up, and quickly realized this was no amateur endeavor; a fire truck was parked nearby, so whoever was putting on the display must have had a permit.

We weren't the only people who'd followed the sight of the fireworks to their source. It's hard to say, given how dark it was, but probably 40 or more cars were parked on the sides of the road. And people were out, watching and cheering the display.

We, too, got out of our car and not only watched the fireworks display, but, close as we were, also felt it, reverberating through our bodies.

It was beautiful, not just because fireworks always are, but because it was such a surprise.

Fireworks in December.

Lighting up the sky.

Inviting anyone who saw them to come a little closer, take a little break, from the hustle of everyday life. From the extra hustle of the holiday season.

I have no idea who decided to put on the fireworks display, or why. Maybe in celebration of the season, of a birthday, of a special event?

I've been thinking about it ever since that evening, and realized that the "who" and "why" of the fireworks isn't so important.

What's important to me is the simplicity of the event. People saw, and responded to, and took delight from the lovely surprise of December fireworks, without planning or scheduling or deciding we'll do this instead of that.

Sure, our kids gave us the child-like urging of "please?" but it took us only a micro-second to respond "yes!" and turn left, toward something unexpected and touching and lovely, instead of right, toward the familiar and comfortable and planned.

I wonder, maybe this is the real gift of this season: Rediscovering how to say yes, like a trusting child, to a surprising display of beauty when it beckons, unbidden, unpaid for or planned for, like streaming stars of light in a dark December sky.

Like grace itself.

(December 10, 2007)

~♥~

Decipher teenspeak: Hear between the lines

It's commonly said that teens often don't communicate openly with their parents.

But what I've discovered is that they do communicate. It's just up to the parents to translate teen-speak into something that makes sense.

Example one:

On the night before the last day of semester finals, my sixteen-year-old said: "I think I'll make a pound cake."

Me: "WHAT? Don't you have a final to study for?"

Teen: "Yes. But it's been such a long time since I've made a pound cake."

Me: "Actually, you've never made a pound cake."

Teen: "Then it's about time I learned."

I wanted to say, no, it was about time that she learned to put her finals studying first, but then I realized she'd been doing that all week.

Translation from teenspeak: Making pound cake isn't really about pound cake. It's about taking a break in order to not burn out from studying.

Example Two:

On that very same night, while that pound cake was baking and our older teen resumed studying, our 14-year-old was packing to leave on a three-day trip to study manatees in Florida. Once her suitcase was zipped up, she said: "You know, some of the parents are coming to see us off."

Me: "Really? Is this a last minute plan for a send-off?"

Teen (shrugging): "No. I've known about it for awhile. I just didn't get around to telling you until now."

This from the kid who re-wrote the packing list because she thought items should be organized by category.

Me: "Uh huh. Well, if you'd like us to come..."

Teen: "Oh no! I'm not asking you to come! I just thought I should let you know in case you want to come. Not that I think you should."

Me (slowly getting it, but unable to resist a bit of teasing): "OK then. I have plenty to do. You don't need me to be there to send you off."

Teen (struggling to keep look of disappointment off face): "That's fine. I mean, I only told you about it in case you wanted to come. Not that I want you there."

Me: "You know what? I think your dad and I will come after all."

Teen: "Well, if you really want to."

Translation from teenspeak: Of course I want my parents there. I want to know you care about me and will miss me. I just don't want to admit that. And I sure don't want my friends to think I need you there.

Example Three:

So the next afternoon, my husband and I went up to the middle school to see our 14-year-old off on her trip. She gave us a perfunctory hug. Which was pretty much what all the teens offered their parents as a good-bye.

Soon, all the teens got on the bus. The parents in the parking lot shivered and joked that we should just go home, since our kids were all merrily pretending we didn't exist anyway.

But then, as the driver got on the bus and started it up, someone's teen gave a little wave. We couldn't tell who it was, so several of us waved back.

Which led to more teens waving. And more parents waving, until the bus pulled out.

My husband and I went home and treated ourselves to our older teen's pound cake, while chortling about the spontaneous wave-a-thon.

Translation from parentspeak: Aw, shucks. As confounding as our teens can be, we love the little stinkers. (January 28, 2008)

~❤~

Infant simulator reveals daughter's responsibility level
Our 14-year-old brought home a baby for the weekend.

Not a *real* baby. A "Baby Think It Over" baby, for health class. The idea is that students take care of an "infant simulator." That's what the manufacturer, Realityworks, calls the "baby."

After awhile, though, it gets tiresome to say, "excuse me while I take care of my infant simulator." So our daughter renamed hers "Ricky."

Ricky came with diaper bag, infant carrier, a cute outfit and blanket, and a sensor our daughter wore around her wrist. Whenever Ricky cried (at various times determined by the little computer chip inside), it was our daughter's job to hold the sensor to Ricky's back to let Ricky know his caretaker was near. Then, she had to figure out if the crying was due to hunger, dirty diaper, or random fussiness.

Ricky also came with special sensor-equipped bottles and diapers. For example, if hunger was the issue, simply putting the bottle to Ricky's mouth stopped the crying and started Ricky "eating." At some point over the weekend, our daughter figured out that the sensor-bottle also hushed crying when placed on Ricky's nose, chin and cheeks.

Which gave us a chance to point out that real infants are a whole lot more challenging than infant simulators.

Still, Ricky-the-infant-simulator proved to be challenging enough.

For example, our first public experience with Ricky was at a fast-food place. I wasn't sure who was more disturbing: the older couple who glared at our daughter, and at us, upon seeing her with the infant carrier and assuming she had a real baby. Or the young worker who was not much older than our daughter, who was disappointed that the infant wasn't real.

But I was quickly distracted by another worker, who served up our burgers while explaining that when she was in middle school, she had the same educational experience, except instead of an infant simulator, she got to decorate a bag of flour and carry it around for three days.

(What does it say about me that my first thought was that, well, at the end, at least she had one of the ingredients for cookies? Never mind. I'm not sure I want to know.)

Then came the first night with Ricky. I went to bed sure in the knowledge that of course I wouldn't wake up when Ricky started crying. Been there, done that. This was our daughter's responsibility.

SHARON SHORT

Yet, two hours later, I was suddenly awake, bolt upright in bed, about to run out of the bedroom to track down the crying baby in the house. About the time I remembered, oh, yeah, "infant simulator," our daughter was already taking care of Ricky.

I guess my ensuing sleeplessness was karmic payback for my earlier thoughts of recycling a flour baby into cookies.

Two more such days and nights passed. Then Monday morning rolled around, and Ricky went back to the health teacher.

Can't say I really miss the little guy. On the other hand, I'm glad our daughter had the experience. And she was so responsible with Ricky, I think she deserves a reward. A non-baby shower, if you will.

Hmmm. I think that calls for cookies.

(March 31, 2008)

~♥~

Just don't ask 'Are we there yet?'
As it turns out, pressing one's right foot into the passenger's side floor board, with enough force to create toe cramps, has no effect whatsoever on a vehicle coming to a full and complete stop.

Likewise, grasping the passenger's side door handle so that both it and one's knuckles crack will not have any impact on the g-forces of a left-hand turn taken too sharply.

What's more, fighting the urge to holler, "no, no, no, slow down, slow down, stop, stop, stop!" only contorts one's face into an Edvard Munch-like scream, which only serves to scare the driver in the car next to yours.

How I have discovered these brilliant traffic truisms?

Is it because:

a. There is an alien driving my car;

b. I've suddenly realized that what the passenger-side mirror really should say is: "Warning: Life (Including Kids Growing Up) Comes At You Faster Than Anticipated;"

c. I am the parent of a teen learning to drive;

d. All of the above

If you guessed "all of the above," then you, too, have probably survived helping a teen learn to drive.

I've anticipated this rite of passage in my teen's life for awhile because the parent has to take quite a few steps before the teen can start learning to drive.

First, there were several chats with our auto insurance company.

Then, sorting out the state of Ohio's temporary license laws, which was like de-constructing some complex algebraic formula.

Finally, we figured out how to get through the paperwork to get the paperwork so our teen could take the temp test to get a little rectangular piece of paperwork authorizing him/her to drive if accompanied by a parent/legal guardian.

All that, before our teen's first attempt to back out of our driveway.

So I guess it's understandable that I really didn't think about how driving is as much a rite of passage for parents as for teens until I found myself strapped in the passenger's seat, screaming "watch out for the lamppost!"

For our kid, learning to drive is a big step toward adulthood.

For her parents, it's a big step toward letting go of the image of her as a young girl and starting to see her as a young woman.

Sure, it'll be a while before she's truly an adult.

Yet, somehow, nothing screams "impending adulthood around the next curve" quit like a teen in the driver's seat and a parent in the passenger's seat screeching "watch ouuuuut!"

Don't worry. The lamp post survived its close-encounters-of-the-teen-driver-kind.

And we're surviving this rite of passage.

In fact, on our last jaunt out, I was so relaxed I started to turn on the car radio.

The driver, however, informed me that I shouldn't create distractions.

This from the same kid who used to say, from the back seat, while I was driving in heavy traffic: Mommy, turn around so I can show you the picture I just drew!!!

Oh, that's right. Must remember she's not that little kid any more.

It's probably just as well I can't turn on the car radio while my daughter is driving.

I have a feeling that no matter what station I tuned into, and no matter what it was playing, I'd hear Fiddler on the Roof's "Sunrise, Sunset."
(April 7, 2008)

~♥~

Old fear is now just water under the bridge
"But weren't you nervous, watching her race?" my friend asked, incredulously.

I was a little taken aback by my friend's question, a result of my description of watching my oldest daughter's first rowing competition.

A little background: my daughter became interested in rowing a few summers ago. Last summer, she went to a week long rowing camp with the Greater Dayton Rowing Association. She enjoyed that experience enough to spend this past winter conditioning for rowing, and then to participate in the junior crew's spring season.

Fast forward to a few weeks ago, and my description of my daughter's first regatta experience... also my first experience of actually seeing her in a row boat.

I told my friend about how surprisingly beautiful a regatta is to watch. How surprisingly passionate my daughter is about rowing. How much joy I felt in watching her row because she's so joyful about it; how natural she looked during the race; how peaceful she looked while rowing with her teammates after the race back to the dock.

Since my focus was on sentiments such as "peace" and "joy" and "passion," my friend's question about my own fear in watching the regatta threw me for a second.

After all, in describing the overall event, I'd also talked about the safety-consciousness of my daughter's coaches, who emphasize proper techniques and water safety. And I'd mentioned that, in fact, I'd observed how safety-conscious the rowing community in general seems to be. (Medic boats, for example, are always out on the water during practices and events.)

So why that question about my being fearful? Why, there wasn't any reason at all to be fearful! And then it hit me.

I suddenly recalled how reluctant I'd been to look into rowing opportunities for my daughter, finding any excuse possible to put it off, even though my daughter kept asking about rowing. I'd confided my reluctance to this same friend. Plus, I'd confided how fearful I personally am around water and how I've struggled to keep knowledge of that fear from my daughters, because I don't want to impose my fears on them. I'd told my friend that, even so, I really didn't like the idea of my daughter doing a water sport.

Even a water sport that's in a boat. With other people in the boat. And floatable oars. And medic boats nearby.

No wonder, after all my fearful whining months ago, that a few weeks ago my friend asked if I'd been fearful watching my daughter row, because I'd predicted that that's exactly how I'd feel.

And yet, the very first time I watched my daughter in a regatta, I literally forgot to be afraid for her. My lack of fear had nothing to do with the safety precautions of the coaches and volunteers (as much as I appreciate those precautions), and everything to do with how happy and peaceful and right my daughter seemed in that boat as she rowed by with her teammates.

So back to the question my friend asked: "Weren't you nervous, watching her race?"

I smiled and finally answered: "No. Not in the least."

My daughter's learning to row, row, row a boat.

And the further I go, not-always-so-gently down the parenthood stream, the more I learn that you can't choose who your kids are or what they'll end up loving in life, but you can choose to love them for who and what they are. (May 19, 2008)

~♥~

Giving her pause: bookstore purchase triggers customer's hot flashes

Recently, a friend sent me via email a how-many-menopausal-women-does-it-take-to-change-a-light-bulb joke. Answer: just one. Because, the answer goes on, no one does anything around here anyway, and… the answer devolves into a hilarious rant with increasing furor and font size.

It was a funny joke about a stage of life still in my foggy future, but after I had a good chuckle, I thought, hmmm. Maybe it wasn't too soon to do a little more serious reading on the subject.

So, I went to a never-to-be-named location of a never-to-be-named bookstore chain, and stood in front of the health section, scanning for titles about menopause.

After a few moments, an eagerly helpful early-20s-at-most young man trotted over.

"Anything I can help you find, ma'am?" he asked.

Normally, I'd find this kind of customer service quite charming.

But instead, I was horrified. No way would I say to this male young enough to be my son, "Why sure! Read any good books lately on menopause?"

So I said, "I'm just browsing!"

And then I hurried over to the next section, which happened to be cookbooks. Perhaps because this was starting to feel a bit like a situation that called for comfort food, I picked up *500 Best Muffin Recipes*!

Never mind that I've been perfectly happy making muffins from mixes—or buying muffins at the bakery—for the past three decades.

But by then the so-young-could-be-my-son sales associate had, thankfully, disappeared. I went back to the health section and found a book by Gail Sheehy: *The Silent Passage*.

Then I went to check out, where I was helped by another man who was much closer to my age. He rang up *500 Best Muffin Recipes!* Then he started to ring up *The Silent Passage,* but paused to comment loudly: "Hey, this is a great book on menopause! My dad got the first version for my mom years ago, and it made life around our house a lot easier! I'm going to get a copy for my wife eventually!"

Whereupon young-enough-to-be-my-son happened by, saw me, saw *The Silent Passage,* got a look of sudden understanding, turned almost as red as I already was, and trotted off.

So, here's what I wanted to say to the older guy: "Hey, pal, what is your problem? It's supposed to be the SILENT passage. Get it? SILENT! Keep blabbing my business to the world, and I will whap you upside the head with my new *500 Best Muffin Recipes!* cookbook so fast you'll be seeing blueberries instead-a stars for weeks! But since we're on the subject anyway, you wanna know how many menopausal women it takes to change a light bulb? Just one, pal, 'cause…"

Etc. etc.

What I actually said was a muttery: "Oh. Great."

Later that night, while whipping up some blueberry muffins from scratch (hey, I bought the book… might as well try one of the recipes) I found myself thinking "wait a minute." Maybe instead of being annoyed at the older, louder sales associate, I should be annoyed at myself.

Why was I so easily embarrassed by buying a book on menopause?

Is it because we live in a Sex-In-The-City culture (yes, saw the movie and loved it) that, nevertheless, still sees the subject of menopause as a bit taboo?

Or is it just my problem?

It may take 499 more muffin recipes before I figure that one out.

In the meantime, I think I should forward those menopause jokes to some of my friends.

(June 30, 2008)

~♥~

Proud to serve a $100 tomato

I mentioned a few weeks ago how much more I'm enjoying gardening, which is true. And I'm even having some success with it, which is also true, at least in the flower beds around our house.

So, I decided I'd also try vegetable gardening, yet again. After all, what better way to change your perspective on the essentials of life than growing your own food?

Now, I've documented past attempts at vegetable gardening.

There was the year I tried to grow cucumbers, over-fertilized them, and ended up with green baseball bats.

Then, last year, I tried growing zucchini, which is supposed to be the easiest vegetable to grow. But last year was also The Year of the Missing Bees, so my zucchini plants' blooms didn't get properly cross-pollinated. I had to break down, go to the farmer's market, and buy zucchini.

Now, that really stung.

Anyway, this year I had a brilliant idea. I'd grow tomatoes! After all, tomatoes are the perfect summer vegetable, except when they're being questioned by the government as potential salmonella-carrying Killer Tomatoes.

At the beginning of June, I carefully planted my little tomato garden in the one sunny patch I could find in our shady yard. The four tomato plants looked so perky and promising!

I fertilized the tomatoes—but just a little. I don't want a bunch of red volleyballs, after all.

I had a personal encounter with a bee which reassured me that pollination would not be an issue this year.

And then I waited patiently.

More experienced gardeners than I (which would be just about any gardener) have assured me that patience is key in gardening. It's certainly a trait I've always needed to develop.

So when one tomato plant was knocked over by something—perhaps an animal running through the yard at night?—I mourned its loss, but I was so glad I had three other tomato plants.

Then another tomato plant bit the dust—literally. I forgot to water during a dry spell.

But I still had two tomato plants left, and I watered those carefully.

Still, a third tomato plant shriveled up. I'm really not sure what happened to it. Perhaps it just missed its neighbor tomatoes and went into shock.

Well, at least I have one tomato plant left, I thought, until, lo, a green orb appeared at the end of one of its stems.

I'd already suffered so much tomato trauma, that I admit, I wasn't thinking straight. I had heart palpitations worrying about over this strange growth. Could tomatoes get warts? Life-threatening warts?

And then I realized the green round thing was... a baby tomato!

I've pampered that tomato plant ever since. As the tomato grew, the scrawny plant leaned toward the ground, until my surviving tomato plant resembled a variation of Charlie Brown's Christmas tree, with a one red ornament making the whole thing plop over.

But, finally, that tomato ripened!

Proudly, I picked it.

I served it to my family.

And tried not to think about the fact that this was, in fact—after my investments in bags of dirt, four tomato plants, water, fertilizer, and medicine for my bee sting—a $100 tomato.

Instead, I decided that that just made this tomato... gourmet.

See? Growing your own food really does change your perspective.

(August 4, 2008)

~♥~

SHARON SHORT

194

CHAPTER 8

~❤~

Just Ask an Amoeba

We all need challenges, just ask an amoeba

Recently, I ran across a news clip about a scientific experiment involving amoebas.

Amoeba lovers, don't fret; this scientific experiment did not involve testing medicines or eyeliner on amoebas, or injecting them with illness-inducing strains of, well, other amoebas, or withdrawing amoeba food or amoeba sleep.

In fact, the scientists created the perfect amoeba environment. So, what happened to these amoebas floating around in the perfect, stress-free environment?

They died.

Just sank right down to the bottom of their perfect little 5-star Petri dishes, and keeled right over.

I'm not sure how a shape-shifting blob keels over, exactly, but the results of this surprisingly cruel experiment are fascinating; so fascinating, in fact, that I wish I could have interviewed one of those amoebas as it sank to the bottom, its little pseudopods flailing hopelessly.

Me: Excuse me Mr.—or is that Ms. Amoeba—

Amoeba (sighing): No need for formality. Just call me Amoeba.

Me: Oh, OK. So, Amoeba, I don't get it. Why are you and all your amoeba buddies just giving up and dying? You had everything you could possibly want or need!

Amoeba: Sounds great, doesn't it? That's what we all thought when we signed up for this gig. And, yeah, we had it all. The perfect saline solution. No worries about running into ravenous plankton. An all-you-can-eat bacterial buffet. Even twenty-four-hour access to our all our favorite cable channels. Everything from CNN to BFN.

Me: CNN? BFN?

Amoeba: You know, Central Nucleus News. Binary Fission Network. Although that last one was late-night, adults only.

Me: Right. Well, if your life was so perfect, what happened to make you all start dying?

Amoeba: That IS what happened! Life became too perfect. No struggles mean no challenges. Sure, who doesn't need every now and then to kick back, relax, float around, and sip on a glass of Algae Cabernet? But after awhile... boring.

Me: So, you're all dying of boredom?

Amoeba: I think it's more accurate to say that we're dying because our purpose was taken away.

Me: Your purpose was to avoid plankton, eat bacteria, and split up with yourselves!

Amoeba: Hey, don't knock it! So we amoeba aren't much in the industry or creativity areas. We still have a basic purpose. When that purpose was fulfilled *for* us, instead of *by* us, then our purpose ended and so we just gave up.

Me: Hmmm. You know, I see a correlation between amoeba and people. People need purpose, too.

Amoeba: Uh huh. Like torturing amoeba by creating perfect worlds for them?

Me: What are you, a sarcastic strain of amoeba?

Amoeba: Actually, I'm a Pelomyxa palustris.

Me: Oh. Anyway, human purpose takes various forms—competition, creativity, seeking knowledge, helping others. And there are all kinds of ways that purpose manifests itself.

Amoeba: Would that include creating imaginary conversations with amoebas?

Me: Hey, I've learned a lot from our little chat! Why, if even amoebas need to be challenged in order to achieve purpose, then that need must be part of all life… wait, where are you going?

Amoeba: This conversation has been enough of a challenge to inspire me. Forget sinking to the bottom. I'm floating back to the top and demanding that the all-you-can-eat bacterial buffet be removed!

Me: Are you getting rid of CNN and BFN, too?

Amoeba: Don't be ridiculous.

(October 13, 2008)

~❤~

Our family is destined to have a blue Christmas.
I'm not talking economically or emotionally. Or even decorating preferences or the Elvis Presley tune.

I'm talking hair. Blue hair. On my teenaged daughter.

I blame this turn of events on text messaging's inability to convey sarcasm.

You see, a few days ago, I received this text message from our oldest teen: "Plan to dye hair blue. OK?"

I texted back the following reply: "Oh, sure!"

What was I thinking?

That after nearly 17 years of being my kid, this child would know to correctly interpret my reply as a sarcastic: "Oh, right; do you honestly think I'm going to give you permission to dye your hair blue via text message?"

Of course, after nearly 17 years of being her mom, you'd think I'd know that she'd leap at the chance to interpret my "oh, sure!" as a non-sarcastic: "Of course, honey, you have my full permission to dye your hair any color you wish, because obviously something like radically changing your hair color doesn't merit a full discussion."

My only defense is that the combined stress of middle age, parenting, and trying to keep up with communication technology has worn me out.

To be fair, before the actual dying took place, we did have a conversation about (a) the permanence of the color change—my teen had already researched a dye that washes out after a month, and (b) the reason for her desire to turn her locks blue—turned out, she'd made a pact with a few friends that they'd dye their hair blue if their band did well in the season's final contest. The band did; thus the urgent need for blue hair.

Of course, I could have explained that the "oh, sure!" wasn't actual approval, and told her, no, she couldn't really dye her hair blue. I could have given her all kinds of reasons.

People will stare!

What will everyone think?

The holidays are coming and we can't have family photos with a blue-haired teen!

But then I got to thinking… if you can't experiment with your looks in outlandish ways when you're young, when can you?

And then I thought about all the issues I *could* be dealing with as a parent of a teen. Temporarily blue hair seems pretty minor in the scheme of things.

Next I thought, oh, who cares what people think? It's her hair. She can share her reason for going blue, or not, as she wishes.

But the final reason I agreed to the blue hair was, in fact, thinking about those holiday photos.

Someday, her future spouse or kids will be looking through our old photo albums, and come across this Christmas's photos, including ones of our daughter with blue hair. And she'll get to tell this cool story about how she got away with dying her hair blue as a teen.

Of course, what I'm really looking forward to is the possibility of her future kids saying, "Well, if you got to dye your hair blue, then why can't I (fill in the blank)..."

If that happens, I'll be sure to send my future grown daughter a message (via whatever has taken texting's place) that says: "Hang in there, honey, and you'll appreciate the joy—and humor—of being a mom."

And I won't mean that sarcastically.

(December 1, 2008)

~♥~

Can you hear me now? Only if you're a teen

A few evenings ago, my kids said they wanted to show me something "interesting" they'd run across on the Internet.

I hurried to the computer, both excited and anxious. Excited—oh, boy, they're researching college scholarship opportunities! Anxious—uh, oh, in doing that research, they discovered something super nasty...

Of course, if I hadn't been so excited and anxious, I might have noticed my daughters looking at each other and giggling. What couldn't they wait to show me? A site called ultrasonic-ringtones.com.

I learned from the site that these ultrasonic—a.k.a. mosquito—ringtones operate at a frequency that only kids under the age of 20 can hear. The site includes a fun little hearing test, with tones from 8kHz to 22.4hKz. 17kHz and up is supposedly just for the under-20s.

Of course, my kids wanted me to take the test.

Of course—sucker mom!—I took it.

Of course, the highest I could hear was 12kHz. The "test results" button offered this charming message: "You're in a mid life crisis. Your ears aren't what they once were and you have resorted to doing online hearing tests."

That led to a demonstration by my darling children of their ability to hear a 21.1kHz tone, with this cute "test results" message: "You are a dog. Or maybe you are a mosquito, you certainly can't be human."

This in turn led to my kids' giggles evolving into outright laughter, which in turn inspired the dog to start barking. Both of which I heard perfectly well.

I didn't say a word.

I simply launched my silent-but-deadly mom-arched-eyebrow-of-doom. Apparently, though I obviously can't hear it, my mom-arched-eyebrow-of-doom also transmits at 21.1kHz or above, because both the kids and the dog hushed up right away.

The next morning, after the kids had left for school, husband for work, and the dog was still happily snoozing, I engaged in a little more research into these ultrasonic ringtones.

Turns out, according to the BBC, that the ringtones evolved from a "deterrent device" featuring the high-pitched 21.1kHz tone, used to drive teenage troublemakers away from a theatre in a town in England.

Of course, teens have now cleverly figured out a way to use the tone in a nefarious anti-adult plot: ringtones that only they can hear.

I wondered... what if I turned-the-tones for my own nefarious plot? Sure, teens can hear these ultrasonic tones. But for some reason, they are utterly deaf to "wake up!" or "dinner's ready!" or "clean your room!" even when repeatedly shrieked at high decibels.

Why, I could record the ultrasonic tone and instead of shrieking "wake up," sneak up on my kids and play the ultrasonic tone right by their ears. Hah! Who's laughing now?

I went back to the ultrasonic-ringtones.com web site. I couldn't resist taking the test just one more time.

And guess what! This time—with no laughing teens, barking dogs, or end-of-day weariness—I could hear the 19.9kHz tone... not quite the level of my kids, but the test result's message this time was: "You aren't even a teenager yet! Your hearing rules! You're either quite young or you've looked after your ears."

Somehow, this new result significantly improved my mood. I abandoned my nefarious plot to use the ultrasonic tones against my teenaged kids.

After all, I can always wield the silent-but-deadly mom-arched-eyebrow-of-doom.

(January 26, 2009)

~♥~

Unflappable GPS unit sets example on road of life

I just got a GPS for my car! It's the coolest thing: all I have to do is program in the address of where I'm going, and somehow through the magic of space satellites, the GPS on my dash board knows how to provide directions! Why, it even speaks aloud: "At intersection, turn left..."

Fine, go ahead and laugh at my enthusiasm. I know GPS is not exactly news-breaking technology. But I've never been an early adopter of technology. Except one time. Remember the Commodore 64 personal computer?

Yeah. Exactly.

Since that one early-adopter experience, I've been one of those wait-and-see purchasers of all things techie. Plus, new technology is always the most expensive when it is first introduced.

But GPS seems here to stay, my husband found a great deal on a GPS unit, and I'm tired of always getting lost. (I always think I'm heading north, and should hang a left, no matter what the directions or map says. This means I spend a lot of time going around in circles.)

So, now we have Aunt Bee—as in Aunt Bee from "The Andy Griffith Show"—in my car. Why did we name our GPS? We just have a habit of naming things in our family. Plants. Cars. GPS systems.

Anyway, I have to say I love Aunt Bee! Aunt-Bee-the-GPS has made my life much easier. And I'm so much less dizzy, since I'm not going around in circles now.

But I also have to admit... after about a week of always knowing where I was going, the charm of Aunt Bee started to wear off a little. She was just so, well, bossy.

So I started to wonder, what would happen if I turned "left" when Aunt Bee said "turn right at the next intersection."

Would she get annoyed? Would her little electronic voice chirp: "I said turn left, you ninny. What do you think you're doing?" Would her unit start to quiver on my dash? Explode from frustration into a little pile of springs and wires and plastic bits?

Before I could go any further with my imaginary anthropomorphizing of Aunt Bee-the-GPS, my opportunity to find out came up.

Aunt Bee said, "At next street, turn right."

So I turned left.

Ha! Take that Aunt Bee!

Except… now I wasn't quite sure how to get back en route to my destination…

And then Aunt Bee said, "Recalculating. At next street, turn left…"

No matter how many times I ignored Aunt Bee's directions, she just chirped: "Recalculating" and gave me a new set of directions.

In some ways, "recalculating" seems like a good philosophy in life right now.

I'm on my same basic path, with my same basic goals that I've had since my early twenties. But I'm at a different place now than I was when I started out with those goals… back before GPS was even around. I'm not just older; my perspective is different now, too. The world around me has changed quite a bit, and right now, it feels to me—and to many others, I suspect—like it is in a stage of major flux. My kids are growing up. My dog is graying.

All this makes it tempting to think, "Panicking!" Or, "retreating." Or just plain "*stop!*"

But I rather like "recalculating."

After all, it's easier to get where you want to go when you're not going around in circles.

(March 16, 2009)

~♥~

Happy birthday, Dad, and thanks

A few weeks ago, I asked my Dad what he'd like for his birthday. He was about to turn 85-years-old.

Dad just shrugged and said, "I don't need anything."

I said, "OK, how about something you'd *want*, then?" I started listing off clothing, electronics, and gardening items, and each time, Dad would just shrug and say something along the lines of, "I have everything I need."

Truth be told, I knew I could get him some… *thing*—another cap or sweater—wrapped it up nicely, give it to him for his birthday, and he would smile and said thanks.

But, somehow, I didn't want to get him some… *thing* for his 85th birthday that he wouldn't really need. Or want.

Then, for some reason, I thought of… baseball. I knew Dad liked listening to Reds' games on the radio or watching them on TV. Since we didn't go to sporting events when I was a kid, I assumed his interest in baseball was a later-in-life development. I'd never heard him mention going to a professional game, or wanting to.

Still, I found myself blurting out the question: would Dad like me to take him to see the Reds play on his birthday, for his birthday gift?

And I waited for him to answer that, no, he didn't really need to do that.

But he surprised me. He lit up, grinned, and said, "Sure!"

So, on his 85th birthday, we went to The Great American Ballpark (which, frankly, will forevermore in my heart remain Riverfront Stadium.)

Our seats were high behind home plate, which agreed was the best way to watch a game. We got to the park early enough to have hot dogs for lunch while waiting for the game to start. After we finished our hot dogs, another question popped into my head. I asked Dad if he'd ever played baseball.

The second I asked it, I thought it must be a silly question. After all, Dad grew up in Appalachia, on a tobacco farm, in a time and place far removed from Little League.

But Dad said, "Oh, yes! Sometimes we'd get a stick for a bat and a hedge apple for a ball and find some field and play the sun went down."

After that, the game started, and we were caught up in following it. The Reds won, 8-2, over the Braves. Dad liked the fireworks. I told him he was good luck for the Reds.

Later, I thought about the young boy, long before he would be a dad, playing ball in a grassy field with a stick and a hedge apple. And I thought about the 85-year-old man, watching his first major league game. In some ways, such stark contrasts between the boy and the man, the grassy field and the major league ballpark, the pick-up game and the professional game.

But in some ways, no contrast at all. The boy knew, and the 85-year-old man knows, that experiences, and sharing them with loved ones, matters more than some… *thing*. Than any… *thing*.

And somewhere in the middle of my life, I'm trying to both remember, and re-learn, that.

Thanks for that birthday gift, Dad.
(May 4, 2009)

~♥~

Parenting milestones give as much as they take
I recently took our daughter on round two of college visits.

On one of the campuses, I had a distinct sense of déjà vu. This was not particularly surprising. By then, I'd lost count of the number of ivy covered buildings I'd seen. The quirky campus icon—usually a rock, seal or bench—I'd observed. If only I looked a few decades younger, I could lead a college tour myself, giving the ubiquitous spiel: we-have-wifi-and-microwaves-are-allowed-in-the-dorms-and-this-is-the-best-school-ever!

Then I realized… I really HAD been on this particular campus before… while pregnant with the daughter I was now accompanying on this college visit.

For a little while, I let my mind wander from the perky tour guide's commentary, and remembered I had attended a weekend-long mystery writing conference on this particular campus.

During the luncheon, I was seated next to one of the author/teachers. He congratulated me on being pregnant and we chatted a bit about young family wife. I was carrying our first child; the teacher and his wife had two children, a baby and a toddler.

The conversation then moved on to mysteries and writing and the conference. At the end of the luncheon, though, the teacher looked at me and said: "People will look at you and say, oh, you're about to have a child— THAT will certainly change your life. And often they will say it sarcastically, like this is a bad thing. But you and your husband decided to have a child because you wanted this change, and you wanted to experience life as a parent. So don't let anyone make you feel like you will be missing out on something better because you're having a child."

I thought his comment was sweet—but a little odd. Until a few weeks later, back at work, someone said to me almost exactly what he'd predicted: "You're going to have a kid? Well, your life will never be the same again!" And in that sarcastic tone that implied my life was somehow ending, rather than taking a new turn.

I just smiled happily and said, "No, it certainly won't!" in a cheerful way.

As I walked near the back of the college tour group with other parents—our daughter and other prospective students were, eagerly and appropriately, at the front of the group—I thought about how funny it was that in some way both my daughter and I had made this trip full circle.

She'd first been at that campus a few months before being born; I'd first been there a few months before becoming a mom. Now she was back a few months before deciding where to apply; I was back with her, thinking about how much life we've both lived and experienced in the 18 years since we first visited. And about how, as she and her sister grow up and launch out on their own, all of our lives will change.

I suppose someone could say to me: "Your firstborn is getting ready to leave home in a year or so? Well, your life will never be the same again!"

And the comment could be construed as a positive prediction... or a negative one.

But I've learned that at major milestones, life doesn't end. It just takes a new turn. That's true for parents of kids leaving home, and for the kids who are leaving.

So I hope I will just smile and say, "No, it certainly won't!" with as much cheerfulness as sentimentality.
(June 22, 2009)

~♥~

Photos rule summer before senior year

We're at the height of summer, and I know I should be sipping lemonade and enjoying the moment.

Instead, I find myself awash in photos. Our oldest kid is about to enter her senior year, so this summer, she needs to have her yearbook photo taken. She says she doesn't really care about a yearbook photo, but I do: I don't want to be the mom whose kid's yearbook photo is an empty head outline.

But while scheduling the yearbook photo, I learn that a *yearbook* photo and a *senior* photo are no longer same thing—showing up in a nice outfit, posing for the photographer, and purchasing several copies of the photo. Oh, sure, one *can* still do it that way—but now the custom is to do a separate senior photo session that can include: multiple outfits, multiple poses (both indoor and outdoor), props (sports gear, instruments, pom-poms—whatever represents the senior's activities.)

Our darling senior says her yearbook photo will serve just fine as her senior photo, but I don't want to be the mom who can only show off one pose of her kid, while all the other moms have twenty.

So I arrange the senior photo session. Our darling senior draws the line at two outfits (one casual, one semi-dressy), no props, indoor poses only. However, before the photo shoot, I try to sneak a trombone, rowing oars, art supplies, and the dog into my car as props, but I'm busted when the dog bays. Our darling senior points out that she doesn't need props to be herself in her photos, and makes me put them all back.

Even without the props, the session goes well. So well, that I suggest we buy at least a hundred copies of every pose. But our darling senior makes a list of folks who she thinks would actually appreciate having a copy of her senior photo, and we purchase accordingly.

Which seems to be more than enough photo-management for one summer... except we then learn that our darling senior's marching band collects childhood photos of the seniors for various senior activities.

We're instructed to pick seven photos.

I start loading up boxes with various photo albums of our darling senior because I'm pretty sure that "seven" is just a minimum. And I definitely don't want to be the mom who sent in too few photos.

But while I'm still fussing over whether or not we should get copies of the yearbook photo as back-up senior photos, our darling senior gets to Daddy. Before I know it, Daddy has picked out childhood photos of our darling senior. Seven, to be exact.

At this point, our other darling gets into the photo game.

I find Little Sis contemplating our two "photo clocks," one for her, one for her sister. Around the big middle "school days" oval are smaller ovals, one for a picture from kindergarten through 11th grade. The "school days" oval gets filled in with a senior picture.

Little Sis says softly: Big Sis's clock is almost filled in.

I gave little sis a hug. I find our darling senior, give her a hug too. Locate husband reassembling photo albums and hug him too. Even hug the dog.

Serve up lemonade to everyone (except the dog; he gets a treat and fresh water.)

And then I… relax. Ahhh.

I don't want to be the mom who forgets, every now and then, to live in the moment.

(July 6, 2009)

~♥~

Cats exercise urge to prey on unsuspecting items

Our cats have never been great hunters. That could have something to do with the facts that (a) they are indoor cats and (b) we endeavor to keep all things huntable outdoors.

Still, I've never been convinced they'd been good hunters outside, either.

Example A: A few years ago, a confused bird flew in our house just as I opened the door to get the newspaper. After I chased the bird out of the house, I realized our cats had serenely watched from the couch the spectacle of me running after the bird, making encouraging comments about how it would be so much happier outside: *Aieeeee! Get out! Get out! Aieeeee!*

Once I slammed the door and my ruffled feathers settled, I caught my cats looking at me with expressions that clearly stated: What?

Example B: The other day, a bug wandered in while I carried in groceries, apparently thinking I was in a mood to share. I wasn't. After I disposed of the bug, there were my cats, standing in the kitchen door. They were looking at me with expressions that clearly stated: Did you remember the moist kibble? Preferably the tuna flavor...

So it is no wonder that we were all baffled, at first, when socks started appearing at the bottom of our stairs.

Well, actually, I wasn't baffled at first. I assumed an errant sock had fallen off the top of a laundry basket.

But the next morning, I got up, started downstairs... and saw another sock, waiting for me at the bottom. I knew no one had done any laundry, so the sock hadn't fallen off the top of a basket en route to the upstairs bedrooms.

This was a dirty sock. And by that I mean a really dirty sock. I recognized it as one of my younger daughter's running socks. So for a second I considered that perhaps the sock had taken on a life of its own, and was sloughing its way up from the laundry room (hey, I hadn't had coffee yet) but then I realized that the sock was not moving.

And then our cats peered around the corner. Their expressions clearly stated: We have brought you a sacrifice. Please feed us some of that yummy tuna kibble.

I couldn't believe it. For years, these two cats ignore home-invading birds and bugs, yawn in the window sill at squirrels line-dancing in our front yard and they suddenly decide to become mighty hunters? By leaving sock sacrifices at the bottom of the stairs?

Well, I decided to put a lid on it. Literally. That night, I went to bed knowing that clean laundry was put away, and dirty laundry was in lidded baskets.

The next morning, there was a knit glove at the bottom of the stairs. The glove could only come from one place: the winter wear box. Which was at the back of the coat closet. Whose door was still firmly shut.

The cats' expressions: Oh, yes. That happened. What now?

I hurried to the kitchen to prepare their breakfasts.

By now, it's part of the morning routine to see what "sacrifices" the cats have left for us at the bottom of the stairs each morning. The dog's squeaky toys. Mementos that were stored away in sealed boxes on the top of basement shelves. And every now and then something that makes one of us exclaim: hey, I was looking for that!

To which the cats give looks that say: you're welcome. Now feed us.

(July 20, 2009)

~♥~

SHARON SHORT

Kid No. 2 speeds along

Parents of more than one child don't *mean* to take parenting the post-first-born child(ren) less seriously… but somehow, we end up being more relaxed with them. And occasionally—if we're being honest—more lax.

For our first child, I filled an entire photo album with pictures of just her first few months.

For our second child, I took a few photos, and bought an album, which I'm pretty sure we still have. Somewhere.

I've always figured our second-born didn't mind our more relaxed approach with her. I've always comforted myself that as a result, she's a pretty relaxed person herself. And I've always thought of that as a benefit for not just her, but for the whole family.

Until she started to learn to drive.

We made our first child practice endless hours in a nearby parking lot before letting her drive on main roads. Months passed before we allowed her to attempt the highway, and even then—with both parents micro-managing her every maneuver—she got on at one exit and, a minute and a half later, off at the next.

With our second child, we had about four practice sessions with her in that empty parking lot before driving sessions on main roads. And sure enough, she became a confident driver more quickly than big sis.

So, on a recent mom-daughter trip, when she asked if she could drive on the highway, I said "sure." I would never have said "sure" to such a request from her big sis so early in her driving.

In any case, we swapped seats at a rest stop. I talked her through entering the highway, as well as a few lane changes. She was doing just fine, so I started to relax, and pretty soon, I drifted to sleep.

And when I woke up, she was merrily driving along— over the speed limit! By two whole miles per hour!

Suddenly, as our lives flashed before my eyes, I realized what an error I'd made all these years, being so relaxed with kid No. 2. This was the direct result of letting her get away with uneven pigtails in elementary school, when kid No. 1 always had to have perfectly even pigtails! Of not making her eat all her peas at dinner time!

End result of a lifetime of relaxation? Kid No. 2 was a speed demon!

But it wasn't too late, I reasoned, to tidy up my parenting style with Kid No. 2. So I had her slow down and get off at the next rest stop, where we again swapped seats.

For the next five minutes, we argued back and forth. To her, I was "freaking out" over her going 57-miles-per-hour. To me, I had long been a too-lax mama with kid No. 2 and needed to make up for it, a.s.a.p. Uneven pigtails and skipped peas were one thing, but being relaxed about learning to drive? No way! This was too serious!

And I told her as much. For good measure, I added, just wait until you're teaching your kid to drive on the highway! You'll know how I feel!

To which kid No. 2 gave me her best are-you-nuts look and said: no I won't, because there's no way I'm teaching my kid to drive on the highway after she's only been driving a month. That's what driving schools are for!

What could I say to that?

I put the car in gear, entered the highway, and thought, uh huh. Just wait until she has kid No. 2.
(August 3, 2009)

~♥~

Time for daughter's dreams

We finally bought our youngest daughter her own desk.

Since she was a little girl, her desk was a hand-me-down--my desk from when I was a kid, circa 1970-something.

It was a corner desk, antique white, with gold paint trim—the dream desk for girls back then. I covered the inside of the drawer with hippy-dippy blue and green flower shelf liner. Perfection!

And, years later, not a bad hand-me-down desk for that girl's little girl.

But eventually it became apparent that the desk wasn't really functional for a 2000s teen. No notches or curves in the back or sides for computer cords. Not designed for keyboards or computer screens. And after awkwardly placing a computer on the desk, no real space for books or homework.

We put off replacing that desk as long as possible… but finally, for our daughter's sixteenth birthday, we gave her the gift of picking out her own desk.

It's much more functional. Just-right cut-out for computer monitor. Perfect space for keyboard, plus homework, books, an iPod, CDs and cell phone.

I have to admit, I expected to feel all sentimental about my old desk becoming a relic, something that might be interesting to refinish and use in an odd corner to display a collection or a vase of flowers, but no longer functional as a desk.

But I wasn't sentimental at all. I told myself it was because I've embraced the technological changes that necessitated an up-to-date desk. Or that I'm really not as sentimental as everyone tells me I am. (Hah!) Or that it was because I was just so relieved that we got the desk together with minimal bruising of thumbs and egos, and no spare parts left over. (This latter is actually, I'm sure, part of my uncharacteristic lack of sentimentality.)

But then, a few hours after our daughter's new desk was assembled in her room, and my old desk was relegated to a dark basement corner to await its fate, I walked past our daughter's room, and caught her carefully arranging her desk. Should the funny frog sculpture go between the computer speakers on the shelf over the monitor? Or was that a better spot for framed photos of family and friends?

Catching that glimpse of our daughter, so intent on making those decisions about how to place things on her new desk—*her* new desk, not a hand-me-down from mom or from anyone else, but *hers*—made me understand why I wasn't sentimental.

It was time—long overdue, in fact—for her to have her own desk, her own space, and not just for technological or practical reasons. Just as I remember forming my identity at my desk—all that time spent scribbling stories in notebooks! Dreaming big dreams!—she needs to do the same, in her own space.

And yet… when I noticed that she'd pulled the hippy-dippy blue and green flower shelf liner from my old desk drawer to re-use in her new drawer, I had to smile.

It's nice to know that in any generation's desk, there is, after all, a little room for just a dollop of sentimentality. (November 30, 2009)

~♥~

CHAPTER 9

~♥~

Zipping Down the Bunny Hill of Life

Making cookies, memories

Recently, I have been on a mission to simplify aspects of my life. For example: making fewer varieties of Christmas cookies. And making the easier kinds—certainly nothing involving a rolling pin or cookie cutters!

Actually, I haven't made cut-out cookies in years. So much easier to whip up some drop cookie dough. Or visit the Pepperidge Farm aisle at the grocery.

But, when one's 17-year-old, high school senior daughter says: "Mom, let's make gingerbread people this year!" there is only one possible course of action.

Dig out the old gingerbread recipe.

Pull out the rolling pin.

And try to remember just where I stored those cookie cutters.

Eventually, I find our cookie cutters. They're in the back corner of a top cabinet in a box leftover from the first toy my husband and I ever purchased—soft blocks for the very 17-year-old high, high school senior daughter who wants to make gingerbread people.

I spread the cookie cutters out on the counter and immediately spot the gingerbread boy and girl cutters.

It would be practical—certainly, it would fit the mission of simplifying—to pluck out the two necessary cutters, and quickly tuck the rest back in the toy box.

But instead, I stare at the cutters.

I'd forgotten about so many of them.

And about so many memories associated with them.

Take the tree, the angel and the bell. For some reason, I was inspired to buy those while I was in graduate school. I vaguely remember thinking the cutters were cute, picking them up at the grocery: my first cookie cutters!

I got carried away and made too many sugar cookies. (I was single and living solo then.) Then I had an inspiration: I'd take some over to the apartment across from mine, to the elderly, grandmotherly lady who lived alone, and seemed lonely.

She was so delighted, and I accepted her invitation to come in for tea and a visit. I can't remember what we talked about, but it doesn't matter, and it didn't really matter then. I was a bit lonely myself, and a little overwhelmed trying to figure out my new solo life. What I do remember is that we had a grand time.

Months later, when I was moving out to go to New Orleans for my first professional job, and the grandmotherly lady, who had taken ill, was moving to a nursing home, her daughter stopped me as we were both carrying out boxes from the apartments and told me how much it meant to her mother that I'd brought over cookies the previous Christmas.

I was a little surprised. After all, I thought *she* was the one being kind by accepting my cookies and offering me tea and talk.

That's the story of the first three cookie cutters. After that, I added to the collection with…

"Mom!"

I look up.

There's my daughter, ready and eager to make those gingerbread people. I know we'll chat while we bake. Years from now, we won't remember about what. But that won't matter. It will be enough to remember we had a grand time.

Further trips down memory lane can wait.

It's time to make a new memory.

But I pause just a moment before getting started, thankful for the reminder from the cookie cutters that simplifying doesn't mean giving up the sweetest, simplest pleasures in life.

(December 21, 2009)

~♥~

Courage and inspiration found on a bunny hill

Several weeks ago, our 16-year-old casually mentioned a new MTV show called "The Buried Life."

The concept is simple: four 20-something guys made a bucket list of 100 things they'd like to do before they die. Then, they went around the country doing them, and for each item on their list, they help someone achieve something on his or her list.

When our 16-year-old brought this show up, it was in that "oh this doesn't really matter" tone that teens use when something actually does matter to them, but they don't want to be too obvious about it.

So I replied with, "Huh, sounds interesting; guess I could watch it with you" in that "oh this isn't that big of a deal" tone that parents use when they sense a chance to spend time with their kid, but don't want to blow it by being too obvious about it.

It turns out that the show is fun and inspiring—so inspiring, that our daughter and I made our own lists.

Which both happened to include skiing.

The down hill kind.

Which our daughter decided to take seriously. Which our other daughter and my husband also thought sounded like a fun family adventure.

(Have I mentioned before that my husband and children are all athletic and fearless... and I'm the exact opposite?)

But there was no way I was going to look at my 16-year-old and say: "Aw, I was just kinda kidding about that skiing item on my bucket list, and I'm not doing this with you."

Thus it happened that I found myself—a non-athletic, physically risk-averse, middle-aged, not particularly fit woman—at the top of a ski slope.

Utterly terrified.

Completely clueless—even though we took a ski class.

Finally, though, it was clear that the 5-year-olds on the bunny hill were getting annoyed with me, and I'd have to go down on my own or they'd push me down.

So I told myself—I had to do this. For my daughter. For my friend who has cancer who told me I can do this, who lit up with a big smile and said, "Skiing makes me feel so fully alive!" For my other friend who used to ski and do athletic things, who now fights MS.

I held the images of these people in my mind, took a breath—and went down that hill.

Then fell, tumbling butt over head.

The 5-year-old pros on the bunny hill thought it was hilarious.

Our 16-year-old quickly progressed to the medium hill, and then the challenge course, skiing with big sis (the only one of us who'd skied before.) My husband did just fine on a beginner hill.

But I—knowing my limits and being realistic—stuck to the bunny hill—determined that by the end of the day, I'd make it down, without falling.

And, finally, I did.

I actually skied down without falling four whole times!

And while I can't say I fell in love with the activity, or ever felt that "fully alive" sense my friend mentioned (I stayed in the oh-thank-God-I-didn't-break-a-leg range of emotion), I did realize, after awhile, that I'd transitioned from being determined to do this on everyone else's behalf and became determined to do it, just for me.

Which, in itself, is a pretty "fully alive" feeling.

And just goes to show that courage and inspiration can be found even on a bunny hill.

(February 22, 2010)

~♥~

Lenten sacrifice prompts family to try vegetarianism
A few days before Lent, Oldest Daughter said during lunch: "What would you think about becoming vegetarians for Lent?"

We were having hamburgers.

Husband gave his hamburger a tenderly loving look, and then said: "You mean… give up meat? All meat?"

Oldest Daughter replied: "We could still have fish. Lots of vegetarians include fish in their diets."

I said: "Well, if we could still have fish, that doesn't sound too bad. We love fish!"

Youngest Daughter said, aghast: "Fish… every day?"

I said: "Of course not! We'd want variety. There are lots of vegetarian foods. Like… chocolate!"

Husband added: "And ice cream!"

Me: "Sushi!

Husband: "Cheese pizza!"

Me: "Eggs!"

Husband: "Baked beans!"

Me: "French fries!"

We'd have kept going on like that for awhile, but Oldest Daughter jumped in: "Mom! Dad! The whole idea is to not only give something up as a sacrifice—but to try healthy foods we normally wouldn't have."

Husband and I gave each other a look: wow, see what happens when the kids turn into young adults? But Youngest Daughter misinterpreted our shared look as confusion.

So she clarified: "I think what sis means is… if you're going to be vegetarian, you're going to have to eat vegetables."

Me (a bit offended): "We do!"

Well, not at this particular meal. Unless catsup counts as a vegetable. Which I adamantly think it does not.

Oldest Daughter: "Sure, we have veggies as side dishes... but the idea is to truly try to be vegetarian."

Husband, looking at Youngest Daughter (now back to happily munching her hamburger): "What do you mean, if 'you're going to be a vegetarian...' Aren't we all doing this?"

Youngest Daughter: "Are you kidding? I'm going to the grocery and getting a steak!"

Still, both daughters had a point. Being vegetarian would mean cooking, serving, and eating vegetables... as the main dish.

It's only been a week and a half, but so far we've learned a lot about going the vegetarian route.

I put out a "help!" plea on Facebook, and received lots of good tips and recipes.

I thumbed through my own recipe collection and found that, actually, I have quite a few vegetarian recipes that I've just neglected.

We went to the library and checked out some excellent vegetarian cook books.

We ate out at one of usual restaurants—and discovered that eating vegetarian there was quite a challenge. So we're looking forward to trying, or revisiting, several restaurants that offer more vegetarian options. (Sad as it is, one can only eat dessert as the main course so many times.)

We've come across a philosophy, in one of the cook books, that the vegetarian style of eating means switching from the mentality of one main course and several supporting sides, to thinking of a meal as several dishes, all of equal value.

We've gone to the organic section of our grocery. Giggled at a few things. And decided to try a few others.

So, rather than being a drag, something to get through, this "let's be vegetarian for Lent" experience is fun. And tasty! So far, anyway. After all, we have about four and a half more weeks to go.

But Youngest Daughter hasn't run out to buy a steak just yet.

(March 1, 2010)

~♥~

It's finally mom's turn to have a little fun

Even though I'm actually a few years away from being an empty nester, I've been wondering for awhile—well, ever since both our daughters entered high school—just how to go about making the transition.

And since our oldest graduated high school… and our youngest became an upperclassman… I've REALLY been wondering.

The answer came about as the best answers to such questions do: unplanned, unresearched, and unexpected.

A friend sent an email to me and a few other friends: "Hey, let's get together for a girls' night out! Let's go to the two-dollar Tuesday concert at the Fraze pavilion!"

Immediately, I thought of all the reasons why I couldn't/shouldn't.

Behind on housework.

Kids might need help with… something. (Truth be told, I couldn't think of what, in particular, they'd need help with, but old mom-habits are hard to break.)

Gardens could use some weeding.

Probably should spend some time working ahead on work projects, just in case someone needs help with… something… that might end up putting me behind schedule if I didn't work ahead…

And that last thought seemed so convoluted, so over-the-top, that I actually heard the little voice in my head saying: "Oh, for pity's sake. Stop taking yourself so ridiculously seriously! And go!"

Just as I was about to go out the door, my kids stopped me. Not because they needed help with something. But because they wanted to know: "Where are you going?"

That's when it hit me—I knew I was going to the Fraze, but I'd been in such a hurry, I hadn't paid attention to the detail in the email stating what we were going to hear. Or about who all was going.

So I said: "Out. With friends."

The look on my daughters' faces, I realized, was a frustrated mirror of my own expression when I have to dig for details about their activities. So, when the little voice in my head said, go on, tease 'em, I did, adding: "To do stuff. And I'll be back... sometime!"

Then I giggled and dashed out the door before they could press for details.

It turned out that a total of six of us gathered to hear Touch, a fantastic Motown cover band from Dayton, Ohio. As the music started, I began to feel the rhythms in my bones, to remember what it felt like to just forget about duties and responsibilities for awhile and have fun. And when my "adult" inner voice suggested I should just sit still and listen, I ignored it and heeded my "kid" inner voice, reminding me again to lighten up and have some fun.

I guess my friends were listening to their inner-kid voices, too, because there we were—six women all of the same age, who had made it to mid-life with our senses of humor (and rhythm) intact after various health, relationship and work challenges that our children have yet to face. Dancing in our seats. Singing along when encouraged by the band. Giggling with each other at our fabulous selves.

When I got home, my kids asked: so... what did you do?

I grinned, threw my hands up in the air, boogied down the hallway, and crooned off key.

Not even eye rolls could stop me. I kept on-a-boogying: the perfect means for making the "empty-nest" transition!

(June 28, 2010)

~♥~

Pies good, memories better

My oldest daughter and I decided to make an apple pie together a week or so ago.

We've made plenty of pies together before. Apple pies. Pumpkin pies. Chocolate pies. Rhubarb pies. Blackberry pies.

And I've always felt a wee tingle of pride in crafting pies with both of my daughters, both in the camaraderie of making the pie and, I admit, in a secret little pleasure at the idea of my daughters someday making pies with their kids or nieces or nephews or friends and saying: now this is how to make a pie, just like mom used to, just like mom taught me!

This particular pie-making session started out just fine...

Until we started to peel the apples.

As usual, I got out the paring knives, and began paring an apple, and expected my daughter to do the same.

Instead, she opened the utensils drawer.

"What are you doing?" I asked.

"Looking for the vegetable peeler," she replied. "Just look at all the waste you're making with the paring knife!"

"No, I'm not."

"I'm using the peeler."

"But it's for *vegetables*!" I exclaimed.

My daughter just sighed... and did it her way. And danged if the little stinker didn't manage to peel her apples leaving more apple intact.

"My way's quicker," I said, a bit petulantly. She smiled.

My rosy-glow future picture of "this is how mom taught me..." was getting a bit shadowy.

We then mixed sugar, cornstarch and cinnamon, and poured it on the peeled-by-various-methods apples. I reached for a wooden spoon to stir the sugar mixture into the apples, but as I did that, my daughter picked up the apple bowl and started bouncing the apples.

"What are you doing?" I asked, holding the wooden spoon out to her.

"This will distribute the sugar more effectively."

And... she was right. (Although I think if I tried that technique, my apples would bounce right out of the bowl.)

My lovely future picture of "this is how mom taught me..." was starting to fray on corners and edges.

Next it was time to mix Crisco, flour, a dash of salt for the crust. I handed her two table knifes, and she started using them, as I'd taught her, slashing cross-wise.

She sighed. "I've never understood why we don't just buy a pastry mixer."

"Why have kitchen tools around you don't really need," I said. And yeah, I sounded grumpy.

She shrugged. "Oh well. I'm going to buy my crusts pre-made, anyway."

I gasped.

And then I saw her teasing smile.

And as we made the crust—with my technique—we both laughed and laughed. It was the most we'd ever laughed, making a pie, and we've laughed plenty over many pies.

When the pie came out of the oven, it was beautiful. Looking at it, tasting it, no one would know it was made with a mix of hand-me-down techniques and new techniques.

So now my lovely future picture has my daughters making pies with some of the techniques I've taught them, some of their own techniques… and that picture makes me smile. The important part of that picture is carrying on a tradition—not specific techniques.

On the other hand, if we're ever blessed with grandkids, when they're old enough, I'm teaching 'em how to peel apples with a paring knife…

(July 12, 2010)

~♥~

Empty nesters indulge themselves... with a nap

Last Sunday, my husband and I suddenly found ourselves alone... with nothing scheduled... and no kid duties of any kind.

Our oldest was off at college. Our foreign exchange student had left that morning. And that afternoon, we bid "goodbye" to our youngest who was leaving on a multi-day trip with her environmental science program.

We soaked in the utter silence of our house for a good ten or so minutes, and then my husband broke it by saying—"You know, this reminds me of something..."

"You mean, life before kids? When we could do anything we wanted on a Sunday afternoon?"

"Why... yes! We could go to a movie."

Me: "Or for a hike!"

Him: "Out to dinner!"

Me: "Shopping!"

We bantered back and forth like that for awhile until we... fell asleep.

That's right. We had a whole afternoon—no work, no kids—to ourselves, and we used it to take naps.

As I groggily woke up a few hours later, I thought, that clenches it: my husband and I are about to enter what I've long thought of as the "Brussels sprouts" stage of life.

I have an acquaintance (we'll call her Sally) who is a few years older than me. Her children are older than ours; in fact, they've long grown up and flown Sally's nest. I asked her a few years ago what that was like for her and her husband, anticipating that my husband and I would be facing this life change soon enough.

Sally said, "Well, after we got used to it being just the two of us again, it turned out we really liked it. In fact, it's great!"

"Really?" I said. "What's so great about being empty-nesters?"

Sally smiled, a sparkle in her eye. "We can do anything we want, and the kids aren't around to complain!"

I lifted my eyebrows. "Like what?" I was ready to take mental notes about romantic evenings at home without being distracted by worries about what five-minutes-late-for-curfew might portend. Elegant dinners out without thinking about getting home in time to pack lunches or help with homework. Even a smooch or two in the kitchen without teens gasping "oooh… gross!" or rolling eyes.

Sally leaned forward and said, as if she was about to share a really juicy secret, "Brussels sprouts."

Then she went on to explain… much to her and her husband's surprise, they'd developed a fondness for Brussels sprouts for dinner. But whenever she tried to serve Brussels sprouts with dinner while their kids were still at home, they'd roll their eyes and groan and moan at the horror of being subjected to the vegetable. Now that their kids were grown, they could enjoy their Brussels sprouts in peace.

I have to say… I'm with Sally's kids on this one. If you do a search on Google for "Brussels sprouts recipes," you will get 360,000 results. They all look awful to me. No amount of butter, salt, au gratins of nuts or cheese, or other treatments could induce me to think "Brussels sprouts… mmmm, they're what's for dinner!"

On the other hand, I understood what Sally was getting at. Eventually, hopefully, partners who are also parents reach a stage where there's more freedom to do whatever one wants with one's partner, unfettered by the responsibilities of childrearing.

Even if that means a candlelit dinner of Brussels sprouts. Or napping.

At one time, the thought of that freedom…of our identities as parents-on-call-24/7 slowly transforming to still-parents-but-not-on-call-24/7 was a little frightening. Kind of like the notion of Brussels sprouts for dinner.

It's funny, though, how a good, long nap can refresh one's attitude.

After our Sunday nap, my husband and I cooked dinner together and then watched a romantic comedy. Without interruption or worrying about anyone except… each other. So, I'm starting to think maybe the Brussels sprouts phase of life has its advantages.

But I may need a few more naps to be sure.

(November 8, 2010)

~♥~

Every person's contribution to a good cause counts

My husband has been singing barbershop music with various choruses, groups, and quartets since our children were toddlers.

It's a wonderful avocation that he loves. Besides creating wonderful vocal music, he gets to be part of a great community.

And the barbershop singing community always seems to be giving back, one way or another, to the greater community. For example, my husband sings with the Southern Gateway Chorus in Cincinnati. This holiday season, the chorus decided to hold a fundraiser for the nonprofit Cincinnati organization, Neediest Kids of All. (Those of you who are Reds baseball fans have probably heard of it.) Since 1952, the organization has provided to kids in the Greater Cincinnati area hats, coats, shoes, clothing, eyeglasses—and beyond these necessities, opportunities for field trips, camp experiences, and other educational opportunities.

Of course, being a bunch of creative guys, these barbershoppers couldn't just pass a straw hat to collect donations. Instead, they came up with a fun competition that played on the all-in-good-fun natural rivalry among the four barbershop singing sections—tenor, lead, baritones and bass, setting up a "penny wars" game.

Each section had its own jar. Coins counted as a positive point, but bills counted as a negative point. So, the idea was to put coins in one's own section's jar to drive up its count, and bills in other sections' jars to drive down its count. The winning section would simply get bragging rights; the chorus would collect a nice donation to give to Neediest Kids of All.

Now, my husband (a baritone) was pretty sure the bass section would win. "Bass singers are known for doing everything in a big way," he said.

"Shouldn't the leads, well, take the lead?" I wondered.

That cute little quip just earned me a flat look. (Barbershoppers are fine with jokes about their avocation… from other barbershoppers.)

Tenors are known for working hard (all those top notes), but they are also the smallest section, so my husband didn't think they had a chance against the much larger bass section.

"What about your section?" I asked.

My husband, who likes to joke that "baritones sing all the leftover notes," didn't think his section really had a chance because (a) it's the second smallest section and (b) it's used to doing just what it has to (those leftover notes.)

At some point after this friendly game commenced, my baritone-singing-baby wondered if I had a few quarters— one of our car's tires needed air.

"Check the change jar," I said.

He looked a little sheepish. Turned out that besides helping drive down points for the bass section with bills, he'd decided to drive up the points for his baritone section with coins.

So… he'd dumped the contents of our family change jar—a good three months worth of coins—*and* his work change jar (probably a half-year's worth of coins) into the baritone jar.

What could I do? All that change vanished for a good cause. So I dug into my coin purse and offered up the quarters for tire air.

The next day, my husband was gloating.

The baritone section had won—beating those beastly basses, leading leads, and tenuous tenors—by a whopping… quarter.

Of course, what matters most is not that my husband's baritone section won the "penny wars" competition, but that the overall chorus found a fun way to undoubtedly drive up donations to Neediest Kids of All.

On the other hand… I really liked my husband's comment at the end of all this.

"Looks like every person's contribution *does* matter. Something to ponder this holiday season."
(December 13, 2010)

~♥~

Life lessons are worth a refresher course
Recently, I had a health scare. On the one hand, I felt confident I would be fine; on the other hand, there was the

teensiest possibility I wouldn't. Of course, even the teensiest-of-such-teensy possibilities manage to loom large in one's mind. In this case, this teensy possibility I wouldn't be fine was sufficient enough that I actually contemplated cleaning up my office and putting files in order. (I didn't get past contemplating, though.)

Turned out... I'm fine! Hurrah! Yippee! Upon receiving this good news, I basked in warm, glowing thoughts about how wonderful life is. About how very, very much I appreciated the support of my family and friends and how much I love them all dearly. I told myself: I'm never going to take anything for granted again, or get annoyed by little things. Why, I'll just focus on the simple, lovely positives of life: a beautiful flower, the aroma of good coffee, a loyal dog, a sunset-streaked sky...

And then I dropped a glass. Darn, that clatter sound was annoying! And what a bummer, having to clean up that glass. Oh, great, now the dog's barking at a passerby. And, oh yeah, that reminds me I need to go to the pet store and while I'm out take care of another pesky errand...

I caught my thoughts, glanced at the clock and realized that my warm basking in the goodness of life had lasted all of about eight minutes.

And that realization made me burst out laughing.

Fast forward to today—my birthday. Happy birthday to me! Hurrah! Yippee!

I am happy to celebrate another one. But I find myself thinking about how quickly my happy-just-to-be-alive glow dissipated and I wonder: aren't I old enough yet to know better?

To know to focus on the beauty and love all around me and not get distracted by the petty?

To know lots of other things, too—like projects always take longer than you think. That ignoring small problems doesn't make them go away; it just means they'll come roaring back as big problems, so it's best to take care of small problems right away. That the love of and for family and friends is by far the greatest treasure. That ice cream on a hot day and hot chocolate on a cold day trump any calorie-counting scheme, which probably isn't going to work anyway. That a shattered glass doesn't really matter, but taking time to share a toast to health and blessings surely does.

Well, I do know all of those things.

It's just that I seem to keep needing to re-learn them.

And I keep thinking I shouldn't have to; that learning a life lesson once should be sufficient.

But now that I've reached this particular birthday, a new lesson is occurring to me: maybe we're supposed to keep learning certain lessons over and over. Get recertified, if you will, in the bits of life wisdom we slowly, painstakingly gain.

I think that's why I laughed at my hubris in thinking that I'd never again be distracted from rejoicing in the beauty and blessings of life... until the glass shattered and the dog barked.

New life lesson: if we're never distracted from seeing the beauty and blessings of life—or from other life lessons we've learned—we'll just start taking those lessons for granted. We need shattering glasses and barking dogs and annoying errands to temporarily distract us because there's humor and joy in learning, and re-learning, and re-learning again the simplest truths of life.

(January 10, 2011—Sharon's 50th Birthday!)

~♥~

Chase those butterflies, daughter of mine
Our oldest child is not coming home for the summer after her freshman year at college.

Yippeee! Woo hoo! Hurrah!

Oh, wait. Those celebratory exclamations don't seem quite right, do they?

Perhaps a bit more explanation is in order.

It's not that we wouldn't love to have her home this summer, or that we have secret plans to turn her bedroom into a sauna room.

In fact, when she went off to college this past fall, my husband and I often said to each other—"It's OK, sweetie.

Before you know it, summer will be here, and she'll be home for the summer!"

Kids *always* come home the summer after their freshman year, right? It's the summer after their sophomore year that they start taking doing things like taking jobs and renting apartments in their college town...

And it's not that she wouldn't enjoy being home for the summer (perhaps especially if we converted her closet into, say, a sauna.)

In fact, she enjoys weekends home and our visits with her at her college.

But...

She has a fantastic opportunity awaiting her this summer. She'll be an assistant to a research team from her college. The team is going to the Canadian Rockies to do research on the migratory paths of butterflies, to assess if there are changes in those paths, and if so, what those changes might/might not say about climate change.

Our daughter leaves with the team about a week after finals, and will return about a week before her sophomore year starts.

Now, I have to admit (even though she reads this column) that my first reaction wasn't purely Yippeee! Woo hoo! Hurrah!

It was partly that, but also a lot of Whhhaaattt?

Then I went to Google maps, plugged in our address, plugged in where she'll be staying, saw how far away and remote that is (the last several steps in the directions just say... slight right! slight left! right! left... with no road names or numbers) and my Whhhaaattt? turned to Wahhhhh!

But just for a little bit. Because I started thinking about this child and butterflies.

Specifically, about when she was five, or so, and we signed her up to play T-Ball. She was very focused at the T, whacking that ball right off the top with all her might. But in the outfield, she was quickly distracted. Inspecting the ants in the grass. Or chasing butterflies in the sunshine.

When following a particular Monarch butterfly took her off the field (hollers from parents and coaches eventually got her back on), we looked at each other and said, "Hmmm. Don't think softball is going to be for her."

But then we said, "Hmmm. Every kid has to follow her or his own path. She might not grow up to love playing softball, but she'll grow up to be passionate about lots of things. Won't it be fun to see what those things turn out to be?"

And upon remembering that, it struck me that this is exactly what we've reared her and her little sister to do: chase butterflies. Butterflies that are dreams and aspirations and adventures... in the sunshine but also when necessary in the rain... and, yes, off the home field and onto fields afar.

So, my Wahhhhh quickly turned to sincere feelings of pride in and joy for her, for how she's going to spend her summer.

Chase those butterflies, daughter of mine!

When you alight home, we'll be here to listen to tales of your adventures. (And I promise, we won't turn ALL of your closet into a sauna.)

And then when you're off again, chasing other butterflies, we'll say: Yippeee! Woo hoo! Hurrah!
(April 18, 2011)

~♥~

!*#@&%#! Now how about that piggyback ride?

I sprained my ankle a few weeks ago. The first thing people ask when they see the Ace bandage wrapped around my ankle is: "What did you do?!"

Here is what I want to say: I was pole vaulting across a roaring river to rescue a kitten stuck in a tree on the other side.

Or... I was dancing the tango and my high heel snapped.

Or... there was this alligator, see, that somehow got into our garage, and while chasing it with a broom...

But, alas, I have no such fun and wonderful explanations for why I sprained my ankle.

Here's the truth: I was walking.

On the way to a Reds' game with my family. Stone-cold sober. In daylight. On a sunny day. On a sidewalk bereft of icy patches, snow or crowds. While wearing my very sturdy walking shoes. And yes, the laces were tied.

Quite simply, I happened to step on an uneven patch of concrete in the sidewalk at the just-right (well, just-wrong) angle to send me sprawling and my ankle twisting.

Ever hear the old saying, you can judge a lot about a person's character by how they react to adversity?

Well, my reaction to this particular adversity was to spew a definitely R-rated commentary at the shooting pain in my ankle.

When my family tried to help me, I just wanted space for a few minutes. After those minutes passed, I declined offers of piggy back rides from my daughters (seriously? I am *not* ready for such a role reversal) although I did take my husband's arm for support. (Not that I actually needed it for support. No sir-ee.) I hobbled on to the game, put my foot up on the empty seat in front of me, and had a beer. (But only because I didn't have my usual bottle of Tylenol in my mom-purse. Yes sir-ee.)

By the time we got home from the game, my ankle looked like it had caught a rogue fly ball. I had to admit that, indeed, my ankle was truly sprained.

Which just made me mad all over again, especially because of course it had to be the right ankle, making driving an issue. I don't like relying on others for help! I don't like cancelling or rescheduling appointments! I don't like taking time off!

Grudgingly, though, over the next few days, I iced my ankle, elevated it, and took anti-inflammatory medicine. As the baseball-sized lump on my ankle slowly reduced to golf-sized, I started reflecting on my reaction to this minor injury.

Why anger? After all, it was just an accident. The molecules of the sidewalk did not conspire to reach out and trip me. These things happen. Acceptance that they do would seem a more mature response. And there are plenty of people who deal with far worse, every day.

Or how about reacting by just flat-out admitting: this hurts! And then graciously accepting offers of pillows, pain killers, chocolate, arms to lean on--even piggy back rides?

The truth is that while being mature and accepting help are great responses to an annoying interruption to one's routine, anger is probably the most honest reaction. At least initially. For a little while.

But now that I've calmed down, and am transitioning toward a more mature attitude about this minor incident, that piggy back ride is starting to sound kind of fun...
(May 16, 2011)

~♥~

CHAPTER 10

~❤~

Watch It, or the Washer Gets Whacked

Yes, kids, your parents are married after all

I am pleased to announce that my husband and I are married. Now, our parents, children, siblings and friends are undoubtedly shocked by this announcement.

After all, as far as they know, we've always been married. Well, for more than half our lives, anyway.

But, truth be told, my husband and I haven't been fully, completely and totally sure that we've actually been married for the past 27.5 years.

Oh, we remember him proposing. Me saying yes. Getting married.

We've checked into hotel rooms, completed legal work, had two children and bought three houses and probably 10 cars (I've lost exact count)—all as a married couple.

We've celebrated every anniversary and shown our wedding album to our children, several times.

All while knowing that shortly into our marriage, for some reason now completely lost to the mists of time, we looked for our marriage certificate.

And couldn't find it.

Which seemed impossible. After all, who loses a piece of documentation that important?

Especially a couple so early in their marriage that they only have some kitchen items, a bike, a stereo, a couch purchased for $17.50 at a thrift store and two boxes of books to keep track of?

Plus, we hadn't lost or misplaced other important documents like passports and birth certificates and Social Security cards.

So we've never been quite sure if we were just goofy and lost/misplaced the certificate, or if we were just goofy and never quite got it.

A few times over the past 27.5 years, we've said to one another—you know, we really ought to make sure we're, well, officially married.

But something would come up to distract us. A move. A baby. A job change. A health issue. A fun vacation. At other times, we'd joke with one another—hey, wouldn't everyone be shocked if we're not married?

And then we'd say... ah, well, maybe we're married by now anyway, through common-law marriage (assuming that law still exists.)

Or we'd say, if we need to get married again, do we want to keep it simple or make a fun blow-out party out of it?

Looking back, I'm glad to realize that when we argued—because sometimes it's hard to go 27.5 minutes without squabbling, much less 27.5 years—neither of us ever brought the possibility that we're not married anyway into the argument.

I'm not sure if we'd have ever gotten around to checking about that marriage certificate, but my husband's health insurance requested a copy of said certificate (just to make sure I'm really his wife). In 27.5 years, no one has ever asked for proof of our marriage—until now.

Anyway, my husband visited the county marriage license bureau to ask if, perhaps, there might be a license on file bearing our names?

It turned out there was. Our license was too old to be on file electronically, so the clerk had to retrieve it from storage... in the basement, far, far back in the creepy corner where the really antiquated records are kept.

My husband purchased two certified copies. One for the health insurance company. And one for us.

We've vowed to one another to actually keep track of this marriage license.

I'm glad to know I'm really married to my husband, after all. But I'll miss all those times I dreamed up fun ways to ask him to marry me, just in case I wasn't.

(May 23, 2011)

~ ♥ ~

It takes wisdom to love a parade

Quick—which comes to mind first when you think of July Fourth? Fireworks? Or parades?

Personally, I love both.

But there was a time when that wasn't quite true, when I would *tolerate* a parade, but really looked forward to the bang, sizzle, pop, ooh-ahh of fireworks during the cooler dark of evening.

Parades, I thought as a kid, were, well, kind of boring. Even the Macy's Thanksgiving Day parade, after a few larger-than-life characters had floated by on our tiny (by today's standards, anyway) TV screen, became dully repetitive.

Of course, I tend to be a person who likes pageantry of all sorts (parades, fireworks, sports) much better in real-life than captured on TV. But even the first parade I recall seeing in person—a Mardi Gras parade, while living in New Orleans as a newlywed—seemed a little, well, disappointing. Now the pageantry outside of the parade was a completely different story... but I digress. The point is that I figured if seeing even a Mardi Gras parade in real life couldn't make me a parade fan, then I'd never become one.

But my attitude toward parades started changing after my husband and I had kids. Suddenly, I really wanted to make sure our kids went with us to community parades. It seemed important for me to point and say, "Look kids! Firefighters!" Or "Look kids! The football team! The band! The Shriners in miniature cars!"

Never mind that our kids found parades a little, well, boring, and soon became restless for the bang, sizzle, pop, ooh-ahh of fireworks. (One exception: the Sorghum Festival parade in West Liberty, Kentucky, held each September, during which copious amounts of candies are tossed willy-nilly into the crowd, with tossers taking particular care to aim at little kids' feet.)

But of course I never let my kids' protestations stop me from nudging them toward what is good for them. Such as insisting that they put not just one, but *two*, spears of asparagus on their dinner plates. And, eventually, not only attending but actually being *in* parades!

So, for several years, despite protestations of weariness, they marched in a spring festival parade with their Girl Scout troop, because I was both their insistent mother and their fearless Girl Scout leader and I Said So. At first, I tried explaining how much it would mean to people from their community to see them in the parade.

But this was about as convincing as explaining the nutritive value of asparagus spears. So, eventually, I just told them to march on and that they'd somehow miraculously regain enough energy to enjoy the festival after the parade. (And, not really miraculously, they always did.) Since then, they've participated, whine-free if not joyously, in other parades for school activities.

Now, they've outgrown reasons to be in parades. Well, temporarily, I'm sure. I hereby promise to only smile with kindness and understanding—not laugh—if they're ever Girl Scout leaders shooing their charges along a parade route. But for now, though they'll politely watch a parade, I think they still really prefer the bang, sizzle, pop, ooh-ahh of fireworks.

And I still love that too.

But I have also grown, over the years, to appreciate just as much the march, wave, smile, ooh-ahh of a homegrown parade, of people coming together to celebrate all the groups, individuals, teams and organizations that work together to make a community.

(July 4, 2011)

~♥~

So happy to get 'carded'

I got carded the other day! There I was, at the register, the bottle between me and the sales clerk, when she looked at me and said, "Ma'am, I'll have to see some ID!"

I grinned and exclaimed, "Really? Seriously? You're going to card me?! That is so exciting!"

Then I turned around, and said gleefully to the people in line behind me, "I'm being *carded*!"

The pitying/confused/bemused glances of my register-line companions brought me mostly back to reality and the following facts:

1. I'm 50. (I haven't been carded in decades.)

2. I was in line at a cooking ware store. At an outlet mall. (Not at a liquor store.)

3. I was buying non-alcoholic margarita mix. (Not actual tequila.)

So I turned back to the sales clerk and meekly asked, "Why do you need to see my ID?"

She said, "Well, because your credit card is so... old... that your signature has faded on the back."

I burst out laughing at my own pride and momentary confusion, or perhaps at my misplaced optimism that the skin cream I use can not only live up to its promises, but exceed them to the point that someone would think I actually need to be carded.

Then I plopped on my reader-cheaters to help me search my purse for the driver's license that would prove the credit card was, indeed, mine.

While the incident still makes me chuckle, it also makes me wonder just how reconciled I am to this whole time-marching-on thing.

Sure, I do use skin cream. And I like to think my aforementioned reader-cheaters have a cool frame to them and just look like hipster glasses, at least until I peer over the top of the rim.

But I also like to think that I'm sensible enough to accept the joys of the age I am, rather than fight the realities of my age.

No Botox or tummy tucks for me. No wearing the latest teen fashion rage; for example, my daughters can pull the latest fad of feathers-in-hair.

At this point in my life, I'm glad my coif sports just a few grays.

And while I do like some of my kids' bands, they're usually the ones that remind me of Pink Floyd and Queen from my own youth.

And I smile when our teenaged daughters long to get out of the teen years and *finally* become adults.

I remember feeling that way... just wait! When I'm an adult, things will be easier! I'll have more control, more freedom, more time... (Of course, I didn't take into account that with those "mores" came more responsibility, more bills, more accountability...)

It's just part of human nature to chafe a bit about one's age, no matter what it is. And to idealize a different age as better. Youth wish to be older—all that freedom from adult rules! Older folks wish to be younger—all that freedom from adult responsibilities!

For me, I'm just grateful for every day I have had, am having, and will hopefully keep having for awhile.

And my accumulation of years hasn't dimmed my overall optimistic approach to life.

For example, I'm about to take my reader-cheaters on my errand to pick up some tequila to go with my margarita mix. I'll need them to help me find my driver's license in my purse. You know, just in case I'm carded for real...
(September 19, 2011)

~❤~

Have fun! And wear a parachute!

In just a few days, our youngest child will be 18.

An adult.

Just like her big sister who, just a scant nearly two years ago, turned 18.

This, of course, means that my husband and I are now parents of adults.

This fact amuses our children to no end. As in, "hah! We're adults... just like our parents!"

We've accepted their amusement with generous, tender smiles, knowing that just because the clock ticks one minute past midnight, the former 17-year-old turned newly-minted 18-year-old doesn't suddenly know everything there is to know about being an adult. (In fact... there are times we're stilling trying to figure this adulthood thing out... and we've been at it a collective 63 years!)

Now, understandably, our oldest child wanted to give something special to her little sister for her eighteenth birthday. The we-are-both-adults-now sisters wanted to celebrate that fact together.

Awwwww, how sweet, we thought, remembering with sentimentality to the little girls who once shared a secret language during their pre-school years. Who thought they were big-time adventurers by "running away" to the park behind our house. (I didn't let on that I was keeping an eye on them the whole time from the kitchen window.). Who have different personalities and interests and reactions to things and yet who see eye-to-eye on the kinds of things that matter: values, priorities, a zest for life.

Privately, my husband and I tried to guess what our daughters might do to celebrate both now becoming legal adults. We came up with: a shopping spree, a camping trip, white water rafting (sort of scary, but we've done that as a family in the past).

And then they told us their plan.

Sky diving.

As in, going up in the air in a perfectly good airplane.

And then jumping out of it.

For fun.

Most of my friends gasped when I told them of our daughters' plans. A few asked if we were going to 'let' them do this. I explained this was, I'm guessing, partly the point. They've planned the event, our oldest daughter is paying for it as a gift to her younger sister, and since they're both adults, we can't legally stop them.

Oh, I suppose we could try whining and wheedling and try to talk them out of it. But I know that wouldn't work.

And while on the outside I feel an obligation to not be *too* enthusiastic about plans like jumping out of perfectly fine airplanes, secretly, I'm pleased that we wouldn't be able to talk them out of it anyway. And, truth be told, big-physical-wimp though I am, I'm also just a tad jealous of their guts at doing something that sounds both terrifying and exhilarating.

So what we've actually said is, "Well. Have fun!"

I'll quietly hold my breath when they make their jumps. And sigh a prayer of thanks when they land safely.

I'm also under no delusions that once they've successfully achieved this adventure, they won't cook up others. Sigh, say "have fun!" hold breath, sigh prayers of thanks… and repeat. Often. I can tell this is going to be my future as a parent of adult children.

But then, maybe that's the best sign that we've done a thing or two right in rearing our children into adulthood.

They jump out of airplanes… and into life, feet first.

And now the best thing we can say, whatever adventures they cook up in the future, is: "Have fun! And wear a parachute."

(October 24, 2011)

~♥~

Revisiting old fighting grounds

During World War II, my Dad served in the U.S. Army as a Private First Class, 29th Division, 116th Infantry, one of the regiments that took Omaha Beach during D-Day.

Dad had the mumps and missed D-Day. At the time, he was, he says, disappointed. After all, as the only son in his family (his little brother was born while he was in World War II), and because his father was disabled, he could have had a deferment. But he enlisted anyway, taking with him patriotic fervor, shooting skills honed by hunting since childhood in the foothills of Appalachia, and the sense of invincibility that only the young have.

Now, he looks back and says he knows he would have died on Omaha Beach. That he feels sad for all the men who died, although he feels confident that fighting in World War II to rid the world of Nazism was a just and worthy cause.

As it was, he arrived on Omaha Beach and caught up with his unit a month later, just after it took St. Lo back from the Nazis, and put his skills to use as a BAR-man. BAR stood for Browning Automatic Rifle. The life expectancy of a BAR-man on the front lines was three minutes.

But Dad made it through more than a year of intense fighting. I cherish a copy of one of the few photos taken of him during World War II, on his 21st birthday, just before the war ended on the European front. He's standing next to an ox somewhere near the Elbe River in Germany. Dad looks strong and handsome.

During that year, he fought in the battles for Vire and Brest, France, and on into Germany. He was declared missing in action after it appeared to his commanding officer that he'd been blown up, but later rejoined his unit. Wesley, one of his best friends and assistant gunner—like a brother to him—died next to him in battle. Later, in the battle for Brest, Dad was wounded, only realizing that he'd been hit after he helped another soldier to the medic, and that his side was profusely bleeding from mortar shell shrapnel.

For decades, Dad didn't talk much about his war experiences. It was only when our daughters asked their grandpa about his experiences because of a school history project that he started opening up. Carefully editing the stories for young granddaughters' ears. Talking a little more openly with me and my husband.

At the end of this past September, I had the honor of accompanying Dad on a trip back to France to visit some of the sites he recalls from 67 years ago—Omaha Beach, St. Lo, Vire. We also visited Brittany American Cemetery and Memorial at St. James, France, where Dad's friend Wesley was buried.

Dad observed places that only bore vague resemblances to his memories, contemplated lost comrades and the passage of time, studied the stone memorials at various sites to the 29th/116th.

When French citizens—some just a little younger than Dad, some younger than me—thanked him for his service (after seeing his Purple Heart hat), he quietly asked me why they were making such a big deal out of meeting him.

"I was just one soldier," he said.

"But think about what you represent," I replied.

And when a fellow traveler suggested that Omaha Beach should be sacred memorial ground, Dad looked at a young family—a mom, a dad, two toddler-aged children—playing on the peaceful shore, and then said, "No. This is what we fought for. Freedom and peace, so these kids can play."

In honor of this coming Veterans' Day, I say to my Dad—to all veterans—simply this.

Thank you.

(November 7, 2011)

~♥~

Washer whacking

Sometime earlier this year, our washing machine stopped working. The washer filled up nicely with water. But the agitator wouldn't start churning the clothes. Which was, well, agitating.

After all, who wants to deal with a washer full of sopping wet, but still dirty, clothing? The notion of having to pull all those clothes out, dripping wet, and put them in a bucket, and tote the heavy, wet mess to a Laundromat, made me drop the lid and then give it a stern whack with my fist.

Which must have, well, agitated the washer in a whole different way... because it started working just fine.

A temporary fix quickly became a permanent one. It was just too easy to look at the baskets of laundry and think, all right, just get through these mounds of sports clothes, muddy hiking pants, everyday clothes, bath towels, dish towels, sheets... and then we'll research how to actually fix the agitator.

Or hire someone to fix it.

Or buy a new washer.

It was easier to hope that we were just one washer-whack away from the washer fixing itself.

Of course, that didn't happen, so we kept whacking the washer lid. And the washer kept starting.

After awhile, washer-whacking began to seem, well, normal. Even appealing, if one had had a bad day at school or work.

Stressed out by heavy homework load? Impending tests? Job deadlines? Uncertain results? Just do the wash!

There's something so basically satisfying about whacking a washer in those circumstances. No one can accuse you of throwing a temper tantrum for hitting an appliance if it's just to get the washer to start, right? Right!

I can't speak for my fellow family members, but during a particularly frustrating week, I rather wished other appliances would go the route of the washer. I'd have been so much more relaxed if only I'd had a good excuse to kick the oven. Or shake the fridge. Or rattle the dryer. Or choke-hold the water heater.

Even when no one needed to work out frustration via washer-whacking, we were able to rationalize not bothering to actually fix the washer. After all, if we weren't working out frustrations and ready to pounce on the washer with a good whack as soon as the washer filled with water, then it might be awhile before we washer-whacked. Which just meant that particular load got a nice, long pre-soak.

So, overall, not fixing the washer, and letting our temporary whacking fix turn semi-permanent, netted less stressed family members and cleaner clothes.

But then, the inevitable happened.

Whacking the washer stopped working. We tried finding another sweet spot on the lid to whack. We pounded until our fists were bruised.

And finally we had to admit that calling in a professional was the only option.

One repair visit and a hundred bucks later, the solution was found. The hinge on the left side of the lid was out of place. The repairman fixed the lid so it is properly hinged. And now... we can run the washer. Without whacking it.

And I'm grateful.

I think.

I just hope that the washer becoming re-hinged—thus eliminating the opportunity to alleviate stress through washer whacking—doesn't leave any of us, well, unhinged. (December 19, 2011)

~❤~

Fur-tumbleweeds not so bad, after all

"Mom, do we have a vacuum?"

My eighteen-year-old daughter asked me this question just a few weeks ago.

"Is that a comment on my housekeeping skills?" I wanted to know. "On what I have, or haven't, taught you about housecleaning?"

Before she could answer, I headed toward the closet where I vaguely recalled stuffing away the vacuum cleaner. After spring cleaning. During some spring, but not this one. Yet.

The third closet I visited turned out to be the correct one, or so I discovered after digging past garment bags and boxes and rubbing the top of my head, after some random smaller boxes and a bottle of rug shampoo toppled down from the shelf onto my head.

There was the vacuum. Sitting next to it was a rug shampooer. Both cleaning appliances looked a bit forlorn. Dusty.

I should give them a quick once over with a dusting cloth. Assuming I could find one.

Now, it's not that I never clean. It's just that our home has almost entirely hardwood or tile flooring, so most floor cleaning takes place with a regular old broom and damp mop.

The rug shampooer is left over from our previous house. Where, I'm sure, I used that shampooer at least several times. After all, the noggin'-boppin' bottle of rug shampoo was half-empty (which in this case seemed a better way to think of the container than 'half-full.')

As for the vacuum cleaner, well, the pet hair tends to conglomerate in tidy little fur-tumbleweeds. Every time I see one, I marvel at the wonders of static electricity. Every other time, I bend over and scoop up the fur-tumbleweed, and compliment myself for multitasking by simultaneously a. cleaning; b. stretching; c. marveling at static electricity; d. saving actual electricity by not bothering to plug in the vacuum cleaner.

"Mom, I know we have a full-sized vacuum cleaner." I jumped. My daughter was standing behind me, regarding me with bemusement. "I just meant, don't we have a hand-held vacuum too I need to clean out the car. I got dirt in it after track practice."

I seemed to recall a hand-held vacuum, also from our previous house, where we needed it for carpeted steps. Then I noticed a tube poking out of one of the boxes that attempted to concuss me. We checked, and sure enough, there was the hand-held vacuum, but no filters or bags.

We reassembled the closet and went off to the do-it-yourself car wash, which happened to have a very powerful hand-held vacuum. That didn't require filters or bags. And had all of its hoses attached.

On our way home, I was uncharacteristically quiet. Often on such errands I chat with our daughter about her upcoming high school graduation plans. Moving out plans. College plans. Food plans. Dorm plans. Plans for dealing with roommates, laundry, checking accounts...

My daughter correctly read in the silence my sudden worries.

"Mom," she said. "It's OK. You and dad showed me how to use a vacuum. And lots of other more important things, too."

But had we taught her enough? About the *really* important things in life? After all, the big messes in life don't get cleaned up by vacuums or come with bottles of shampoo... My sudden fears were taking over, leaving a vacuum of self-doubt.

Then I noted her bemused smile, her sparkling eyes, her confidence. And, in our newly clean car, I finally smiled, too, as we drove along. She'll be just fine.

Even having grown up with a few fur-tumbleweeds. (March 26, 2012)

~♥~

Volunteer days come to close

My official mom-volunteer days have now come to an end.

Oh, I'll still do volunteer work. And of course I'll still be a mom, helping my kids with specific to-dos if they ask, and always being available for emotional support without having to be asked.

But my days of volunteering to help with kid-activities are now done.

Our youngest child is a senior in high school. So, this track season is her last. So, it was with great sentimentality that in February I signed up for two April volunteer gigs on behalf of her track team: a. cooking up six pounds of spaghetti for the spaghetti dinner traditionally held the night before her high school hosts a relay event; b. work the concession stand at that relay event.

Upon hearing this, our daughter the track co-captain said, "Now, no complaining about cooking all that spaghetti when the time comes!"

That gave me pause.

Had I whimpered in the past about cooking such copious amounts of pasta?

Probably.

But by now, I have it down to an art, or possibly a science. I know how to whip up six pounds of non-gummy pasta in an hour flat, using only two pots, one pasta ladle and zero colanders. And how to keep it warm and not sticky for hours.

From past mama-volunteer gigs for soccer, basketball, taekwondo, rowing, marching band, Girl Scouts, and school events, I also learned how to: efficiently bake 20 dozen muffins for an entire rowing team; organize the sale and distribution of hundreds of flats of petunias, begonias, and so on for a band fundraiser; calm the fears of 22 Girl Scouts during a rain storm on a camping trip and keep the fire going; convince a sandwich shop owner that *of course* he wanted to fulfill a last minute order for a basketball team; keep my head up and my smile wide when a bird decided to leave a deposit in my hair while I was helping chaperone a field trip to an aviary at the zoo...

And so on.

Mostly, all that volunteering (well, except for the bird poop part) was fun. Sometimes, though, looking forward at all the work still to do, it felt challenging... and like there was no end in sight (usually when I was 24 muffins in, with 72 to go.)

As it turns out, our daughter severely sprained her ankle and can't run her senior season, but she is attending as many events as her injury will allow to cheer on her teammates.

And of course I made six pounds of spaghetti and fulfilled my concession stand duty, without complaining.

Well, I do have one complaint.

Concession stand duty came to an early end when the meet was called due to lightning.

Sometimes, looking back, such duties seem to wrap up a little too quickly.
(April 23, 2012)

~♥~

Sometimes, it's sweet to be the filling in the sandwich generation

We hear a lot about the challenges faced by the "Sandwich Generation," those adults who occasionally (or perhaps often) care for their own parents and at the same time their own children.

In fact, the term is so ubiquitous that it became a part of the Merriam-Webster dictionary in 2006. (The dictionary states the first known use of the term was in 1987.) The Sandwich Generation even has its own month (July).

The term also comes with an implication of burden, an image of a beleaguered middle-ager torn between needing to check on a child and, at the same time, on a parent.

And while caring about the health or life issues of both a parent and a child can definitely be worrisome, I made a lovely discovery the other day.

Being a member of the Sandwich Generation can also be a true joy. Even sweet.

Of course, I was sampling cake at the time, so perhaps delectable butter cream icing influenced my assessment.

Just a few days before my butter-cream-induced-revelation, I'd been worried about my dad. He'd had a bout with pneumonia, which he thankfully came through just fine, but he had a bit of a reaction to the antibiotic.

And I'd been worried about our youngest daughter, healing from a sprained ankle.

At the same time, I'd been talking with my dad about having a party with family and his church friends for his 88th birthday.

And talking with our daughter about plans for her graduation party.

Parties, of course, require cake.

Preferably a large, delicious cake, which means a cake not baked by yours truly, but by professional cake-bakers.

So, as dad started to feel better, out went the invitations for his 88th birthday party. And in went the order to my favorite bakery for a beautiful, large, festively decorated cake for his birthday.

Then, about the same time worries about our daughter's ankle started to ease, our daughter said to me... now, you are coming to the bakery with me to meet with my friend and her mom, right? So that together we can figure out graduation cake details--size, decorating colors and style, and so on?

Of course I said... of course.

It turned out that her friend's mom suggested getting our daughters' cakes from the very bakery at which I'd ordered my dad's birthday cake. What's more, she suggested a meeting time that was literally just a half hour or so after I was scheduled to pick up my dad's birthday cake.

So it was that I found myself in a bakery, from which all our specialty cakes (birthdays, graduations, baptisms) have come over the years, double-checking my dad's 88th birthday cake.

And then, minutes later, helping select the details for our youngest daughter's graduation party cake.

I didn't rush either task.

This combo cake errand was one to be savored, enjoyed, remembered, focused upon.

Because it was, yes, sentimental and poignant. But also... sweet. And not just because of the butter cream icing. (May 7, 2012)

~♥~

So long, for now...

"Give us children roots and wings/never fear the change it brings/there is no reason to be sad/be thankful for the time you've had..."

These lyrics are from the song "Roots and Wings" by Stephen Kellogg and The Sixers (Gift Horse album). Since I heard the song a few months ago, the refrain has been playing in my mind, off and on, as we've approached our youngest daughter's high school graduation.

Well, she has now turned her tassel, tossed her cap, received her diploma. We've celebrated with a party, a ceremony, a dinner. And while she's looking forward to a summer with family and friends, I can see in her bright blue eyes an eagerness to move on to the next phase of her young adult life.

Just as her sister before her, she's grateful for and acknowledges her roots. Now, she's eager for her wings.

Several friends and colleagues have asked my husband and me if we're ready to be empty nesters.

And the answer is... as ready as we can be.

We're a little nervous, I'll admit, but we've done a pretty good job staying connected as a couple while rearing our children. We've always understood that our children are a blessed gift, ours to love for all of our lives, but to hold and teach just for a little while.

And as we embrace this change, a bit sentimental but a whole lot excited for the new adventures that await, I'm also welcoming another change in my writing life.

A little over ten years ago, I started writing Sanity Check on a weekly basis. Prior to that, I'd been writing occasional guest columns for this newspaper's Life section. I certainly didn't expect my every-now-and-then pieces to turn into a regular feature, so I was surprised when I was offered the opportunity to write Sanity Check every week.

After just a wee bit of hesitation (writers are always stunned at such opportunities), I jumped at the chance. I'm glad I did. Over the past ten-plus years, I've been honored to share with readers, in nearly 560 columns, my take on the fun and foibles of family life, the grace that follows goof-ups, the humor that saves our sanity in the face of every day stresses and trials.

As our youngest daughter is transitioning to a new phase in her life, the timing feels right for me to do the same in this area of my writing life. My next novel, *My One Square Inch of Alaska*, comes out in February 2013 and represents a new phase of my fiction writing career, telling stand-alone stories from the heart. I also have recently launched a new Sunday column, Literary Life, which celebrates the wonderfully rich literary treasures—writers, book clubs, writing events—of our area. And I've been itching, lately, to write longer nonfiction pieces.

So, today's column wraps up Sanity Check. Thank you for sharing a decade of chuckles and poignant reflection with me. I've collected one hundred of my and readers' favorite Sanity Checks in book format; email me or see my website for details.

I hope to encounter Sanity Check readers as I continue on other literary adventures, so this isn't good-bye, just so long for now. In the meantime, I leave you with this wish from the song playing in my heart and mind: "May you feel your roots and wings/and never fear the change it brings..." (June 4, 2012)

~♥~

ABOUT THE AUTHOR

Sharon Short is the author of the novel *My One Square Inch of Alaska*, which won a 2011 Montgomery County (Ohio) Arts & Cultural District Literary Artist Fellowship and a 2012 Ohio Arts Council individual artist's grant. After a decade of creating *Sanity Check*, she is now the *Literary Life* columnist for the *Dayton Daily News* and directs the renowned Antioch Writers' Workshop in Yellow Springs, Ohio. Short lives in Dayton, Ohio with her husband and is the mother of two college-age daughters. Visit www.sharonshort.com to learn more, contact Sharon, or subscribe to her e-newsletter.

www.ingramcontent.com/pod-product-compliance
Lightning Source LLC
Chambersburg PA
CBHW061426040426
42450CB00007B/917